MILESTONES IN BLACK AMERICAN HISTORY

CENTURIES OF GREATNESS

THE WEST AFRICAN KINGDOMS: 750-1900

Philip Koslow

CHELSEA HOUSE PUBLISHERS
New York   Philadelphia

FRONTISPIECE This bronze mask was created in the kingdom of Benin, renowned for its magnificent wealth and brilliant aesthetic achievements.

ON THE COVER Cast in bronze, these elaborately clothed court dignitaries once graced the royal palace in the kingdom of Benin.

Chelsea House Publishers
Editorial Director Richard Rennert
Executive Managing Editor Karyn Gullen Browne
Copy Chief Robin James
Picture Editor Adrian G. Allen
Art Director Robert Mitchell
Manufacturing Director Gerald Levine

Milestones in Black American History
Senior Editor Marian W. Taylor
Series Originator and Adviser Benjamin I. Cohen
Series Consultants Clayborne Carson, Darlene Clark Hine
Series Designer Rae Grant

Staff for CENTURIES OF GREATNESS
Assistant Editor Margaret Dornfeld
Copy Editor Catherine Iannone
Editorial Assistant Annie McDonnell
Picture Researcher Sandy Jones

First Printing

1 3 5 7 9 8 6 4 2

Library of Congress Cataloging-in-Publication Data

Koslow, Philip.
    Centuries of Greatness, 750–1900: the West African kingdoms/Philip Koslow.
        p. cm.—(Milestones in Black American history)
    Includes bibliographical references and index.
    ISBN 0-7910-2266-8.
    ISBN 0-7910-2692-2 (pbk.)
    1. Africa, West—History—To 1884—Juvenile literature. [1. Africa, West—
History—To 1884.] I. Title. II. Series.
DT476.K67 1994
966—dc20   93-40667
                                                                CIP
                                                                AC

CENTURIES OF GREATNESS

CONTENTS

MILESTONES IN BLACK AMERICAN HISTORY

INTRODUCTION

✳

On a sunny morning in July 1796, Mungo Park, a Scottish explorer, achieved the goal of his long, difficult trek through West Africa and reached the banks of the Niger River. Along the river was a cluster of four large towns. The sight of these settlements, which together made up the city of Segu, dazzled Park as much as the spectacle of the broad, shining river. "The view of this extensive city," he wrote, "the numerous canoes upon the river; the crowded population; and the cultivated state of the surrounding country, found altogether a prospect of civilization and magnificence, which I little expected to find in the bosom of Africa."

Park's account of his journey, *Travels in the Interior Districts of Africa*, became a best-seller in England. But his positive reflections on Africa had little lasting effect on his readers. Later explorers, such as Richard Burton, who harped upon the "backwardness" of Africans, achieved far more attention and fame than did Park, who died during a second trip to Africa in 1805. By the end of the 18th century, European merchants were engaged in a profitable trade in slaves along the West African coast, and any real appreciation of the richness of African culture could only work against them. Nor did the European attitude change markedly in the decades that followed. Exactly 100 years after Park's arrival at Segu, a professor at England's Oxford University was able to write with bland self-assurance that African history before the arrival of Europeans had been nothing more than "blank, uninteresting, brutal barbarism." The professor's remark was published when the British Empire was at its height, and it represented a point of view that sought to justify the exploitation of Africans. If, as the professor claimed, Africans had lived in a state of chaos throughout their history, then the European domination of Africa was surely a blessing. As Europeans imposed their own government, religion, and social system upon Africans, the conquerors could believe that they were doing a noble service.

These views held sway into the 20th century. It was not until the end of World War II in 1945, when Africans began to break away from the European powers and form independent nations, that a sizable group of scholars began to take a fresh look at the African past. As archaeologists (scientists who study the physical remains of past societies) explored the sites of former African cities, they found evidence of a high level of civilization, thus confirming the observations of Mungo Park and other unbiased travelers. Not only had this civilization existed hundreds of years before the arrival of Europeans, but in many respects, the kingdoms and cities of Africa had reached a level of sophistication equal to or greater than that of European societies during the same period. The history of the West African kingdoms offers an intriguing view of a rich and long-neglected world and fascinating evidence of the vast range of human achievements.

MILESTONES
750-1900

✳

c. 750 • The Soninke found ancient Ghana and gain power in the region by making iron weapons. Ancient Ghana emerges as a major trading state in the Sudan, controlling both the salt and the gold trades.

9th century • The Yoruba and Hausa states and the state of Kanem are established.

10th and 11th centuries • Ghana reaches the height of its wealth and power, impressing visitors with the grandeur of its cities. To manage this large kingdom, Ghana's king appoints princes to run its various provinces, creating a system similar to the states of medieval Europe.

1070 • Almoravids, fundamentalist Muslims from the Sahara, invade Ghana.

12th century • Ghana declines as a power in West Africa; the focus of trade shifts to Kangaba, a kingdom in the far south of the former Ghanaian empire.

1221-59 • Dunama Dibbelimi reigns in Kanem, which develops into a major power stretching from Lake Chad to North Africa; eventually the empire becomes Kanem-Bornu.

1240 • Sundiata defeats Sumanguru and becomes king of Kangaba, which grows into the Muslim empire of Mali.

1312–37 • Mansa Musa rules Mali, expanding its wealth and influence. Though respectful of traditional West African ways, he brings experts from Cairo to create Muslim schools and law courts and to introduce new building techniques.

c. 1400 • Dissatisfied with Mali's weak ruler, Gao declares its independence, leading to the rise of Songhay.

c. 1440
- Ewuare becomes oba (king) of the commercially prosperous Benin and unites its people into a powerful empire.

c. 1460-92
- Songhay ruler Sunni Ali, a great general, gains control of the entire middle Niger region, developing new farming methods and beginning a professional navy.

1472
- Portuguese sailors navigate the West African coast for the first time, making contact with Benin.

1493-1528
- Askia Muhammad governs Songhay, instituting Muslim practices and modernizing the government and military; Timbuktu and Jenne prosper as centers of learning and trade.

16th century
- By trading its highly valued textiles and metalwork, Oyo becomes the most powerful Yoruba state and dominates its neighbors. Barkwa Turunda and her daughter, Queen Amina, lead Zaria to dominance among the Hausa states.

1504
- Oba Esigie begins his reign as ruler of Benin and soon establishes a monopoly on trade with the English and Dutch.

1508-1617
- Idris Alooma rules the vast empire of Kanem-Bornu.

1590
- Seeking riches, the Moroccans invade Songhay; they succeed largely because they are armed with muskets.

c. 1695
- A unified Asante kingdom emerges under the leadership of Osei Tutu, who uses traditional religious beliefs to bring his people together.

Early 18th century
- Asante conquers Denkyira and takes over trade relations with the Europeans. The transatlantic slave trade begins to deform the societies of West Africa, depriving their economy of skilled workers and altering the balance of their political systems.

c. 1720-50
- Opoku Ware leads the expansion of Asante, gaining control of the Middle Niger trade routes.

1770-90
- Its leaders hampered by illiteracy, Oyo begins to decline in the unstable atmosphere of the slave trade; by 1840, its fall from power is complete.

1800-1850
- Seeking to create the ideal Islamic state, Uthman Dan Fodio leads the Fulani takeover of Kanem-Bornu and the Hausa states; the Sefawa dynasty falls after a record 1,000 years of stable rule in Kanem. Uthman's son, Sultan Muhammad Bello, unites the Hausa states but shatters the democratic element of the reform movement.

1824
- Provoked by the British governor's attempts to break their control of the region, Asante soldiers defeat the British in battle.

1874
- British forces invade Asante. The Treaty of Fomena, which gives the British free reign along the coast, marks the decline of Asante's power.

1884-85
- The European powers agree to divide up Africa, beginning decades of colonial rule.

1900
- The British occupy Asante, dissolving the last of the great West African kingdoms.

1

THE CRADLE
OF HUMANITY

✳

THROUGHOUT the 20th century, scientists searching for the origins of the human race have turned more and more to the distant past of Africa. Increasingly, they have followed the trail blazed by Dr. Louis S. B. Leakey (1903–72). Based on work conducted in Kenya and Tanzania between the 1930s and the 1960s, Leakey concluded that Africa had been the setting for three all-important beginnings in human history. He claimed, first of all, that the basic stock of primates (an order of mammals that includes apes, monkeys, and human beings) originated in Africa about 30 or 40 million years ago. Then, according to Leakey, the main branch of human ancestors developed from the apes some 12 million years ago. Finally, the earliest members of the human race, *Homo sapiens*, made their home in Africa about 150,000 years ago and gradually spread from Africa to the rest of the globe.

Few scientists would argue with Leakey's first two conclusions; on the third proposition, some scholars contend that the first human beings did not originate in one particular area but in a number of locations,

This skillfully rendered terra-cotta head was found during excavations near the village of Nok, Nigeria, in the 1930s. The sculpture is a product of the so-called Nok culture, which flourished between 900 B.C. and A.D. 200.

Mount Cameroon rises above the grasslands near the Gulf of Guinea, southeast of Nigeria. In dramatic contrast to the Sahara Desert, which borders West Africa to the north, the region at the base of this mountain averages more than 400 inches of rainfall annually.

including the Middle East and Asia as well as Africa. This is a complicated subject, and the issue may be debated for many years to come. However, whether Africa is considered the single starting point of contemporary humanity or merely one among several, its central importance in human history is beyond dispute.

Africa is a huge continent, nearly 12 million square miles in area, a land that has always severely

challenged the people who have tried to put down roots in its vast expanses. The historian Basil Davidson, in his book *The African Genius*, has provided a vivid description of those challenges:

> There are deserts large enough to swallow half the lands of Europe, where intense heat by day gives way to bitter cold by night, and along whose stony boundaries the grasslands run out and disappear through skylines trembling in a distance eternally flat. There are great forests and wood-

lands where the sheer abundance of nature is clearly over-
whelming in tall crops of grass that cut like knives, in
thorns which catch and hold like hooks of steel, in a
myriad marching ants and flies and creeping beasts that
bite and itch and nag, in burning heat which sucks and
clogs or rains that fall by slow gigantic torrents out of
endless skies. . . . There are fine and temperate uplands,
tall mountains, rugged hills, but even these are filled with
an extravagance of nature.

For thousands of years, the first residents of Africa
had no permanent cities or settlements. Instead, they
moved from place to place, hunting wild animals and
gathering plants for food. When the animals moved
to new habitats or the plants in a region died out, the
people were forced to find new locations in order to
survive. The tools they used were made of stone, and
thus the earliest period of human history is now
known as the Stone Age.

About 6,000 years ago, human beings began plow-
ing the earth with their stone implements and plant-
ing seeds that would produce edible foods. Human
beings were able to remain in stable communities,
many of them clustered in the fertile valley of the Nile
River in east-central Africa. Other communities
sprang up to the west, in what is now the vast Sahara
Desert: throughout most of the period from 10,000
B.C. to 2500 B.C., the Sahara was a green and fertile
area. These early farming communities—arising during the period known as the New Stone Age, or the
Neolithic period—were the true beginning of human
civilization.

A great change occurred in the life of these early
communities about 2,500 years ago. At that time,
human beings discovered how to extract iron ore from
the earth: when heated in a fire, the iron could be
shaped into tools and weapons. The coming of the
Iron Age quickly changed the way people lived. Iron
implements were much sharper and stronger than
those made of stone and bone. With iron plows and

RECENT NEOLITHS

PLEISTOCENE PALEOLITHS

iron axes, humans could clear and cultivate larger areas of land than they had previously, and their communities expanded. Moreover, groups that possessed iron spears and swords were able to conquer other peoples equipped only with more primitive weapons. As a result, humanity spread out across Africa: by the beginning of the Christian era, all the

Until about 2,500 years ago, human beings made most of their tools from stone. This display of Stone Age implements is drawn mainly from the Neolithic period, during which humans learned to cultivate the soil.

The features of this Nok sculpture, part of a collection in the Jos Museum in Nigeria, are characteristically graceful and expressive.

regions of the continent were fully settled by the ancestors of modern-day Africans—though the total population of 3 or 4 million was a far cry from the 485 million of the late 20th century.

With the use of iron, society became more complicated. The early Stone Age communities were usually organized into clans—groups based on descent from a common ancestor. The head of the largest clan would often be the leader of the community. Thus the division of society tended to be vertical, with the elder members ruling the younger.

With the coming of the Iron Age, however, a horizontal division of society occurred as well. For one thing, larger communities were often more difficult to govern, so more organization was needed. In addition, people were now performing many different functions besides farming: communities included craftspeople, laborers, warriors, and traders. The inhabitants of Iron Age communities became more aware of their relation to one another and to the outside world. They saw themselves not only as the descendants of their ancestors but also as people who performed a function in society.

A leading example of the change in outlook that occurred between the Stone Age and the Iron Age is provided by remnants of the Nok culture. Little is known about the way the Nok people lived, but their artistic skill is evidenced in the clay figures they left behind, discovered in the 1930s during tin-mining operations near the village of Nok in Nigeria. The Nok sculptures, modeled in terra-cotta, a form of clay that can be heated to a lasting hardness, have been dated by scientists as extending in origin from 900 B.C. to A.D. 200, thus spanning the range of both the Stone Age and the Iron Age.

The sculptures consist mostly of human faces. As Basil Davidson has written in *Africa in History*, "These figures are remarkable for their great artistic qualities, combining . . . a rare sensitivity to human character and features with a sophistication of style that seems extraordinary for the times in which they were made." They show that West Africans had already become vividly aware of the world they lived in, so much so that they felt the need to record their impressions in a form that would last for centuries. This occurred at a time when art was virtually nonexistent in many parts of Europe.

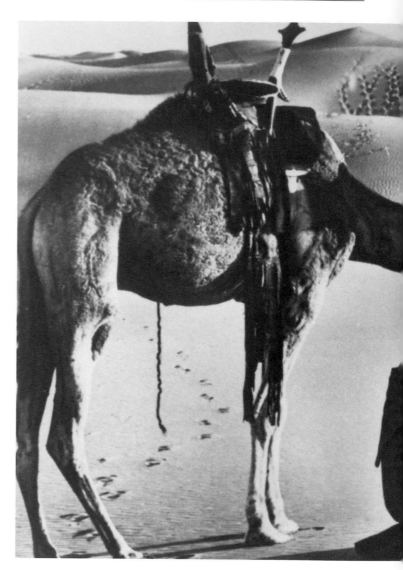

Muslim travelers stop to pray as they journey across the Sahara, the world's largest desert.

Despite the example of Nok, West Africa's location caused it to lag behind the eastern and northern regions of the continent. While West Africans were still living in farming settlements, the Egyptians, in contact with the great river-valley civilizations of the Near East, such as Babylon and Assyria, enjoyed a culture of high sophistication under their rulers, the pharaohs. The communities of North Africa, propelled into close contact with the Romans and Phoe-

nicians by their position on the Mediterranean Sea, were large and prosperous by the 4th century B.C.

West Africa was separated from these civilizations by the Sahara, a 3-million-square-mile expanse of land that, by around 2000 B.C., had dried to desert. This geographic barrier did not prevent the development of West Africa during the Iron Age. South of the Sahara and extending all the way from the Atlantic Ocean to the Gulf of Aden in the Middle

East was a vast plain commonly referred to as the African savanna. Though this plain contained different environments—some dry and open, some moist and wooded—it was, until it merged with dense tropical rain forests along the coast, an area that was both friendly to human settlement and easy to travel through. As the archaeologist Graham Connah has pointed out in his 1987 book, *African Civilizations*, the region's very diversity aided its development:

> Each environment possessed some resources but lacked others. Thus salt was available in the desert and along the coast but was relatively difficult to obtain in the savanna. . . . Thus the forest was deficient in meat but the savanna supported very large numbers of domestic animals. There are many other examples that could be given to illustrate this situation but the important point is that the complexity of the West African environment, as a whole, provided conditions conducive to the development of a complex network of regional trade. . . . It is quite likely that such trading activity was almost as old as West African food production and the beginnings of a trading network could well have been already in existence by about three thousand years ago.

However, one of the most important links in that trading network, the journey back and forth through the Sahara, was truly challenging. Because temperatures in the Sahara, the world's largest desert, can reach as high as 120 degrees Fahrenheit and supplies of water are scant, the trans-Sahara journey required courage, determination, and careful planning. Travelers who became separated from their companions seldom emerged alive.

By the 7th century A.D., trading caravans from North African cities such as Marrakesh, Fez, Algiers, Tunis, and Tripoli frequently made the daunting journey through the desert. Other caravans came from Cairo in the east. The trek became easier when camels began to replace horses, because camels are able to

travel long distances without water, and their wider
hooves make it easier for them to move through sand.
In addition to salt, the caravans brought copper, silks,
and other metalware to the West Africans, who provided textiles, nuts, spices, ironwork, and gold in
exchange.

As the trade routes flourished, the settlements of
West Africa began more and more to resemble their
counterparts to the north and east in size, wealth, and
splendor. Before long, they would be equal to any of
the cities in the world.

2

THE LAND OF GOLD

THE first of the great trading empires to emerge in West Africa was ancient Ghana. Ancient Ghana occupied a large territory that lay between the Senegal River and the western branch of the Niger River. This territory was well inland and thus entirely distinct from the modern-day nation of Ghana, which is situated on the coast, bordering the Gulf of Guinea. Ancient Ghana was founded at least as early as A.D. 750 by a people known as the Soninke; some scholars believe that the date of founding may have been as many as 500 years earlier. In any case, Ghana had emerged as a major trading power by the year 800.

The Soninke originally called their state Wagadu. The term *ghana*, which means "war chief" in the Mande language, was originally used to describe one of the functions of the king. Gradually, no doubt owing to the importance of military power in main-

The homes of ancient Ghana resembled the architecture of this 20th-century African village, constructed of clay and covered with thatched roofs.

Residents of the ancient city of Timbuktu carry goods past a mosque.

taining the state, the term came to replace the nation's original name.

A second title held by the king of Ghana was *kaya maghan*, "master of the gold." The king's two most important functions, leadership in war and control over the gold trade, indicate why the Soninke found it desirable to be led by a single individual rather than a group of clan chiefs. In order to control neighboring peoples, the Soninke needed unified military forces; when dealing with trading partners, it was an advantage to have a unified economic policy.

The power of the Soninke was really based on their superior skill in working iron. Equipped with iron-pointed spears, Ghana's armies easily subdued the forces of their West African neighbors, who fought with much less efficient weapons made of stone, bone, and wood. However, Ghana itself was not the source of the gold eagerly sought by traders from North Africa and Egypt. The precious substance derived from the forest belt to the south of Ghana, where there were rich gold deposits and a population skilled in mining. By controlling the territory that lay between the producers of the gold and those who wished to acquire it, Ghana made itself a crucial element in the trading process.

Ghana was able to control the flow of gold from south to north, and Ghanaians also controlled the north-to-south flow of salt, a precious commodity for which West Africans were ready to trade their gold. For each donkey-load of salt that entered Ghana from the north, the king collected an import tax of one *mitqal,* equal to one-eighth of an ounce of gold. For each donkey-load of salt that left Ghana for the south, the king collected an export tax of two mitqals from Ghana's southern neighbors. In this manner, Ghana became known throughout Africa as the Land of Gold, without itself producing an ounce of the glittering metal.

Ghana also carefully regulated the flow of gold across its borders, making sure that the metal would not become so widely available that the price would drop. As the gold mines of central Europe were being rapidly exhausted, Ghana began to enjoy a monopoly on the gold trade. For this reason, any ruler who wished to obtain gold for the minting of coins could only obtain it from Ghana, by way of the North African traders.

The rulers of Ghana strived to live up to their role as masters of the gold trade, maintaining their kingdom at a level of grandeur that deeply impressed traders and other visitors. Many of these visitors wrote about what they saw, and the most reliable of their accounts were compiled during the 11th century by al-Bakri, an Arab writer living in the Spanish city of Córdoba. In al-Bakri's day, the king of Ghana was Tunka Manin, who, according to the writer, could "put two hundred thousand warriors in the field, more than forty thousand of them being armed with bow and arrow." No less impressive was the splendor of the royal court:

When [the king] gives an audience to his people, to listen to their complaints and set them to rights, he sits in a pavilion around which stand his horses caparisoned in cloth of gold; behind him stand ten pages holding shields and gold-mounted swords; and on his right are the sons of the princes of his empire, splendidly clad and with gold plaited into their hair. The governor of the city is seated on the ground next to the king, and all around him are his counsellors in the same position. The gate of the chamber is guarded by dogs of an excellent breed. These dogs never leave the king's seat. They wear collars of gold and silver, ornamented with metals.

Other travelers reported, perhaps a bit more fancifully, that the king of Ghana held enormous banquets attended by thousands of guests and that he possessed a nugget of gold so large that he could tether his horse to it.

It is likely that the capital city moved several times during Ghana's history, but scholars believe that at the time of al-Bakri's account, the capital was Kumbi

The prophet Muhammad founded the religion of Islam during the 7th century A.D.

Saleh, whose ruins were first discovered in 1914. Throughout the following decades, archaeologists digging at the site reconstructed the outlines of a large city, whose population may have numbered as many as 30,000 people. Like most of West Africa's great trading centers, Kumbi Saleh comprised two separate settlements, one for Ghanaians and the other for visiting North African traders. The houses of the Ghanaians were built in the typical West African fashion, with circular walls of clay and cone-shaped thatched roofs. The North Africans usually built square houses from blocks of stone and finished the interior walls with yellow plaster. In two large mansions uncovered in Kumbi Saleh, archaeologists found a variety of finely made objects, including weapons, farming tools, glass weights for weighing gold, and fragments of pottery.

The upkeep of a city such as Kumbi Saleh, let alone an empire of Ghana's extent, required not only great wealth but also careful political organization. The king might control the gold trade, but with his subjects spread out over so large a territory, there was no way that he could hold all the power of government in his own hands. In order to convey orders, the king had to employ messengers who rode on horseback to far-flung communities. Given the distances involved and the hardships of travel, the network of messengers was not an efficient way of making the most basic day-to-day decisions.

Therefore, the king was obliged to appoint a series of princes to rule the provinces of the empire in his name. The princes had a wide range of power, but they were ultimately servants of the king, and all of them paid taxes to the central government. By instituting this form of political organization, Ghana made a dramatic departure from the previous communities of West Africa, placing itself on a par with the states of medieval Europe.

The rule of Ghana's Tunka Manin was similar in many ways to that of his European contemporary William the Conqueror, the French nobleman who seized control of England in 1066 and crowned himself King William I. Under the feudal system of government practiced by William, lords and vassals were bound together by ties of mutual loyalty. Vassals—in this case the barons of England—held their land by grant from King William; in return, they paid him taxes and pledged to support him in time of war. No baron had the right to wage war on his own, and all were compelled by various legal traditions to pledge their obedience to the king. The same principles prevailed in Ghana, with some important differences. William had invaded England with an estimated 5,000 men at arms, and he would undoubtedly have envied the 200,000 troops at the command of Tunka Manin—not to mention the splendor of Ghana's royal court and major cities.

In the course of history, however, ancient Ghana was not destined to achieve the same longevity as the nation of England. Like William the Conqueror, the rulers of Ghana did not believe in standing still. During the course of their history, they strove with some success to expand their borders. To the extent that they could gain control over both the gold-producing areas to the south and the salt-producing areas to the north, their wealth and power would steadily increase.

Ghana may have enjoyed a monopoly of the African gold trade, but it had no monopoly on the idea of

The Almoravids, who invaded Ghana in 1070, believed in strict adherence to the doctrines of the Koran, the sacred book of Islam. This page of text, a leaf of parchment inscribed in gold, is part of a 9th-century Koran from Kairouan, Tunisia.

expansion. That idea has been the common property of many nations and peoples. In the 11th century, one such group inspired by the dream of conquest was known as the Almoravids. Ghana eventually became their victim.

The Almoravids were as much a religious phenomenon as a political force. They were adherents of the religion of Islam, which had its origins in the deserts of Arabia, to the east of Africa, during the 7th century. At that time, the Arabian tribes worshiped a variety of gods, many of them associated with forces of nature. These beliefs competed with the teachings of both the Jewish and Christian religions, which centered upon a single god and a written code regulating the worship and conduct of believers.

In this context, the prophet Muhammad, an Arab tribesman who spent his early years as a caravan driver, developed the religion of Islam. Like Judaism and Christianity, Islam was based upon the worship of a single god, Allah. Similar to the Old Testament of Judaism and the New Testament of Christianity, the holy book known as the Koran contained the teachings of the new religion, which was in many respects far stricter in its demands upon worshipers.

Like most champions of new ideas, Muhammad met powerful resistance during his career as a prophet. But by the time of his death in A.D. 632, he had gained masses of followers who were eager to spread the faith. By the end of the 7th century, the Islamic Arabs, commonly known as Muslims, had swept through North Africa. In the early years of the 8th century, they crossed the Mediterranean and conquered most of Spain. It was only a matter of time before Islam exerted its power upon the rest of Africa.

The people known as Almoravids were, from the standpoint of the 11th century, newcomers in the Muslim world. They owed their origin to a Muslim holy man named Ibn Yasin, who traveled from Arabia to the Sahara Desert around 1039. Ibn Yasin had been summoned by a tribal leader who wished his people to receive religious instruction. As a fundamentalist, Ibn Yasin preached strict adherence to the doctrines of the Koran, which demanded frequent prayer and allowed very little in the way of personal enjoyment. This teaching was at odds with the general tone of Muslim civilization, especially in North Africa and Spain. In the conquered territories, Muslims had developed a graceful and enlightened culture that featured wide-ranging commerce, scholarship, science, and splendid works of art and architecture. The North Africans had little use for Ibn Yasin's harsh doctrines, and as soon as his sponsor died, they drove the teacher away.

Undeterred, Ibn Yasin traveled to the Atlantic coast and founded a religious community known as a *ribat*. He had great success in attracting followers, who became known in Arabic as *al-Murabitun*, "the people of the ribat," from which the name Almoravid was derived. When he had sufficient forces, Ibn Yasin conquered the Saharan tribes that had once rejected him, and he made himself master of the northern desert. Following Ibn Yasin's death in battle in 1059, the Almoravids eventually split into two groups. The northern group, under Yusuf ibn Tashufin, systematically conquered North Africa and then swept into Spain with the object of controlling the entire nation. The southern group, led by Abu Bakr, set its sights on Ghana.

Abu Bakr began his campaign against Ghana in 1070 by forming an alliance with the people of Takrur, a kingdom on the Atlantic coast. The Almoravids quickly captured and plundered Audoghast, one of Ghana's most important cities, located in the northwestern part of the empire. But Ghana's army was so powerful that Abu Bakr's forces were unable to capture Kumbi Saleh until 1076. By contrast, the Almoravid forces that invaded Spain made short work of a supposedly invincible Christian army at the Battle of Sagrajas in 1086. They seemed certain to conquer all of Spain until the warrior Rodrigo Díaz, known as El Cid, defeated them at the Battle of Cuarte in 1094.

In the end, the Almoravids could not hold on to their West African territories either. The proud Ghanaians staged continual revolts, and Abu Bakr himself was killed while fighting rebel forces in 1087. For two centuries thereafter, a number of neighboring states, including Takrur, tried to gain control of the territory of Ghana. None of their attempts was successful. But throughout all the region's political and military upheavals, the western savanna continued to prosper. It was only a matter of time before a new empire took shape to recapture the grandeur of the Land of Gold.

3

"WHERE THE KING RESIDES"

✳

WHEN the empire of Ghana crumbled under the assault of the Almoravids, the peoples once subject to the king of Ghana were free to pursue their own goals. One group that profited from Almoravid rule, the Soso of Takrur, had ambitions that went far beyond autonomy. When Almoravid power began to decline after the death of Abu Bakr, the Soso were among the peoples who tried to fill the power vacuum in the western Sudan. Finally, in 1203, a zealous Soso leader named Sumanguru seized control of the former Ghanaian capital, Kumbi Saleh, and attempted to form a new empire.

Sumanguru was a powerful figure, reputed to have the gift of witchcraft for use against his enemies. But he soon found his drive for control of the western Sudan in serious jeopardy. For one thing, the Muslim traders who had been installed in Kumbi Saleh for centuries refused to accept his overlordship. They abandoned their settlement and traveled north to the

The village of Kirina, pictured here, was the site of a battle between rival kings Sundiata and Sumanguru in 1240.

edge of the Sahara, where they set up a new trading center at Walata. Thus, Sumanguru lost any chance of controlling the gold trade with North Africa.

An even more significant challenge to Sumanguru's ambitions came from the Mandinka people of Kangaba. Kangaba was a small state situated in the far south of the former empire of Ghana, but it had played an important part in the gold trade. Scholars believe that the Mandinka of Kangaba had journeyed to the gold country along the Senegal River and transported the precious metal to the trading centers of Ghana. In addition, the Mandinka had long been skilled in farming, cultivating rice and other valuable crops in the fertile land occupied by Kangaba. For this reason, their population increased steadily through the years, and their importance in the politics of the region grew.

This shrine is located in Kangaba, a small town on the upper Niger River that was once the capital of the Mandinka kingdom Kangaba. The building belongs to the Keita clan, of which the legendary Sundiata was a member, and dates from as early as the third century A.D.

Like the Muslim traders, the Mandinka found Sumanguru's regime difficult to deal with. His taxes were burdensome, and he failed to maintain law and order in his dominions, with the result that the caravan routes were plagued by bandits. Sumanguru also considered it his privilege to carry off Mandinka women. Kangaba seethed with the spirit of revolt, but the Mandinka's king lacked the courage to lead them. When he realized that Sumanguru was preparing to move against him, he fled and left his people to fend for themselves.

The Mandinka found their savior in the deposed king's half brother, Sundiata Keita. According to oral traditions that still survive in West Africa, Sundiata was born lame but was cured by a miracle, with the aid of the royal blacksmith. He became a great hunter and warrior, but he had to go into exile to escape the anger of the king's principal wife, who feared that Sundiata would rival her own son for the throne. Sundiata now returned home and gathered an army to confront Sumanguru. The two sides met in battle at Kirina in 1240. As the battle is now recalled, both leaders employed their supernatural powers. The army of Sumanguru appeared on the horizon in the shape of a cloud, and Sundiata's army took the form of a mountain.

Sundiata's powers proved greater. He knew that Sumanguru, like all warriors, was protected by magic only against wounds from iron. Sundiata prepared a poison and injected the venom into the claw of a white rooster: when one of the Mandinka warriors shot Sumanguru with an arrow tipped with this claw, Sumanguru's magic deserted him and he vanished from the face of the earth. Sundiata now took control of Sumanguru's former territory and appointed Mandinka leaders to govern the various provinces. The little state of Kangaba now emerged as the center of a new empire, which soon became known as Mali, meaning "where the king resides."

The rulers of Mali adopted the title *mansa,* which means "lord" in the Mandinka language. They occupied the same position as the former kings of Ghana, with one significant difference: the lords of Mali were all Muslims.

Abu Bakr, the leader of the Almoravids, had not merely been seeking riches and territory when he invaded ancient Ghana. He also sought to forcibly convert West Africans to the religion of Islam. Combined with the influence exerted by the long-established presence of Muslim traders from North Africa, Islam had a powerful impact on West Africa, at least among the ruling classes. It is safe to conclude that the majority of the people continued to follow their traditional religions, which had much in common with the religions practiced in the Middle East before the coming of Islam. Nature worship and the belief in spirits were important ingredients of the ancient creeds. Animals were often given the status of gods; in West Africa, the snake and the ram had particular power. For the average West African, these age-old beliefs, centered upon the land and all its inhabitants, appeared to provide greater meaning and comfort than the more complicated ideas of Islam. The notion of a single god who had no real earthly form, not to mention a holy book written in an unfamiliar language, could not have had great appeal to the people of the African countryside.

According to Basil Davidson, the actual founders of West African states, such as Sundiata, well understood the need to combine political achievements with long-held beliefs. In his book *Africa in History,* Davidson points out that Sundiata's conversion to Islam was undoubtedly a gesture of goodwill toward the Muslim traders; to his own people he presented himself as a champion of traditional religion, "a

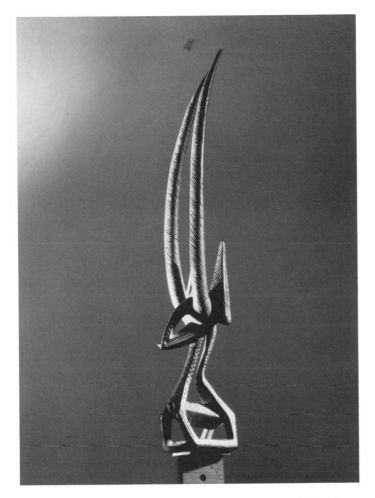

This dance headdress, a creation of the Bambara tribe in Mali, represents Tyi-wara, a mythical figure whose name means "farmer with the strength of a wild animal." Half-man and half-antelope, Tyi-wara is credited with teaching the Bambara their agricultural skills.

powerful man of magic or enchantment." For later rulers, on the other hand, the unifying principles of Islam, and the rich culture that had been built upon it, offered a promise of growth and stability that proved irresistible. Sundiata's successors, therefore, gradually turned away from the ancient traditions. They set about making Mali a great Muslim empire, and they succeeded brilliantly.

Perhaps the greatest of all the lords of Mali was Mansa Musa, who ruled from 1312 to 1337. Under his regime, the borders of Mali expanded

in all directions, encompassing more trade routes, more wealth-producing areas, and the thriving cities of Gao and Timbuktu along the Niger. Consequently, in 1324, when Mansa Musa embarked on a pilgrimage to Mecca, the holy city of Islam, he caused a stir in the Muslim world that gave rise to long-lasting tales of grandeur. He was said to have taken more than 500 slaves with him, each one of them carrying a staff of solid gold. (Basil Davidson points out that present-day chiefs in West Africa still have ceremonial parades with golden staffs, though the staffs are now made of wood and simply decorated with gold.) When the great lord passed through Cairo, he gave so much gold to the residents that the price of the commodity fell and the whole economy of the city was affected.

Mansa Musa's experiences in Cairo and Mecca inspired him to rival the Muslim princes of the East, not only in wealth but also in culture and good works. He returned from his pilgrimage with a number of Egyptian scholars, who set up schools and law courts. The Muslim schools, famed throughout the world for their superb quality, had a major impact on West Africa, where scholarship had not previously been promoted. Because the religion of Islam centered upon the study and observance of the Koran, reading and writing were all-important, and more and more Muslim West Africans began to acquire these skills.

Islamic law courts were also distinctive in applying the commandments of the Koran to every aspect of life. Muslim judges, called *qadis*, possessed wide-ranging powers to inflict punishment, including the death penalty, on offenders. Such strict measures were foreign to the African law administered by tribal elders. In Africa, as in other societies whose religious beliefs are closely tied to nature (such as those of the North American Indians), the death penalty was rarely applied. Even in cases of murder, the judgment usually involved a payment of goods or livestock to the victim's family. Thus, the emphasis was on restoring balance in a practical sense rather than fulfilling a principle of justice: taking "an eye for an eye" might be morally satisfying, but a gift of cattle would put food in the mouths of a family that had lost one of its providers.

Mansa Musa, understanding how deeply his people were wedded to their traditional religion and ways of life, was careful to maintain the old religion and law side by side with the new Muslim institutions. For example, the Muslim traveler al-Bakri noted that there were areas in Mali to be avoided: "Around the king's town are domed huts and groves where live the sorcerers, the men in charge of their religious cult. In these are also the idols and the tombs of their kings. These groves are guarded, no one can enter them nor discover their contents. The prisons of the king are there, and if anyone is imprisoned in them, no more is ever heard of him."

Mansa Musa had brought architects as well as scholars back from Cairo, and before long his builders had erected a magnificent mosque (Islamic house of worship) in Timbuktu and a new royal palace in the capital city of Niani. Mansa Musa also introduced new building techniques for ordinary houses. Instead of the traditional round structures with clay walls and conical thatched roofs, the people of Mali now became accustomed to brick houses with flat roofs.

Like the kings of ancient Ghana, Mansa Musa appointed governors to rule Mali's various provinces. Mali went a step further, though, by surrounding the king with a group of advisers who roughly corresponded to the cabinet ministers of later centuries. In the capital, there was a minister known as the

*The principal mosque of
Timbuktu, built during the
reign of the Malian king Mansa
Musa, is the oldest surviving
mosque in West Africa.*

hari-farma who was in charge of regulating all the fishing in the Niger River; the *sao-farma* supervised all of Mali's forests; the *babili-farma* was in charge of agriculture; and the *khalissi-farma* took care of the empire's financial affairs.

Apparently, most of these officials performed their duties well. The often chaotic and dangerous conditions that had plagued the western Sudan after the decline of ancient Ghana gave way to a reign of peace and prosperity. Ibn Battuta, a Muslim scholar who traveled widely throughout Africa and Asia during the 14th century, visited Mali 12 years after Mansa Musa's death and found that the ruler had created a state of "complete and general safety." At the court of Mansa Suleyman, Musa's successor, Ibn Battuta was confronted by a splendid spectacle:

> The lord of this kingdom has a great balcony in his palace. There he has a great seat of ebony that is like a throne fit for a large and tall person. It is flanked by elephants' tusks. The king's arms stand near him. They are all of gold; sword and lance, bow and quiver of arrows. . . . Before him stand about twenty Turkish or other pages, who are brought from Cairo. One of these, standing on his left, holds a silk umbrella that is topped by a dome and bird of gold. The bird is like a hawk. The king's officers are seated in a circle near him, in two rows, one to the right and one to the left. Beyond them sit the commanders of the cavalry. In front of him there is a person who never leaves him and who is his executioner; and another who is his official spokesman, and who is named the herald. In front of him there are also drummers. Others dance before their king and make him merry.

As he traveled throughout Mali, Ibn Battuta found much more to marvel at, including the beauty and manners of the women, who were treated with great respect and did not follow the Muslim practice of covering their faces in the presence of men.

He also noted that the people of Mali were very free in sexual matters, with married men and women often having "companions" outside the family. The learned traveler wrote:

> A man may go into his house and find his wife entertaining her "companion," but he takes no objection to it. One day at Walata I went into the qadi's house . . . and found him with a young woman of remarkable beauty. When I saw her I was shocked and turned to go out, but she laughed at me, instead of being overcome with shame, and the qadi

said to me "Why are you going out? She is my companion." I was amazed at their conduct, for he was a theologian and a pilgrim to boot. I was told that he had asked the sultan's permission to make the pilgrimage [to Mecca] that year with his "companion" (whether this one or not I cannot say) but the sultan would not grant it.

Compared with this prosperous, cultured, and sophisticated society, 14th-century Europe was hardly impressive. During that period, European life was dominated by the Hundred Years' War, a long series of conflicts between France and England over England's territorial claims in France. The war, which raged on and off between 1337 and 1453, devastated much of France. Meanwhile, all of Europe was swept by the Black Death, an outbreak of bubonic plague that wiped out one-third of the continent's population by 1350. Peasant revolts broke out in France and England; learning and culture declined with the death of Europe's leading scholars; religious life was disrupted and fanatical sects began to flourish as large segments of the clergy succumbed to the plague. Nothing could have been farther removed from the peaceful, prosperous cities of Mali, with their mosques and new brick houses, their markets filled with goods, the canoes in the river Niger, and the great caravans coming in from the Sahara.

As it turned out, much of Mali's stability rested upon the leadership of Mansa Musa. Most of his successors were lesser men. Mansa Suleyman, who ruled during the time of Ibn Battuta's visit, managed to continue the great tradition, but after his death in 1360, the throne was occupied by a succession of rulers who were both inept and unpopular. The strain on the empire became apparent after 1400, when the city of Gao proclaimed its independence and refused to pay taxes to the emperor. At the same time, the ever-dangerous Tuaregs swept in from the Sahara and captured both Walata and Timbuktu. In the west, the Wolof people began to build their own empire. Mali did not collapse; the respect and honor its emperors had earned still remained throughout the western Sudan, even as the empire's power and wealth declined. But after 200 years, it was time for other peoples to occupy center stage—in a process that unfolded, next to the violent convulsions of Europe, like a great historical pageant.

4

SONGHAY

AMONG the great conquests of Mali was the thriving city of Gao on the Niger River. The city had been founded in the 7th century by the Songhay, a race of energetic traders. By the beginning of the 11th century, when the Songhay king Kossoi converted to Islam, Gao was a major terminus for the great caravans making their way south through the Sahara (a position Gao still occupies today). Early in the 14th century, Gao's prosperity made the city a ripe target for the lords of Mali, and for decades its citizens submitted to their rule. But after the decline of Mali's military power, the Songhay people began their own program of expansion. By the time they were done, their empire had become the largest ever known in West Africa.

The rise of the Songhay empire to greatness began in the 1460s with the reign of Sunni (King) Ali, a leader whose deeds are still spoken of in the villages of West Africa. Sunni Ali was

The city of Jenne, situated on the Bani River, a tributary of the Niger, was taken by the Songhay leader Sunni Ali in the 1470s. Long established as an important trading center, Jenne flourished throughout the Songhay empire, serving as a link between the traders of Timbuktu and the gold producers of the southern forest belt.

above all a great general, and his skills as a commander were in constant demand. While the Songhay had been subject to the king of Mali, their tax payments had at least purchased peace and stability. Now, with Mali's forces no longer present to maintain order, the Songhay were pressed on all sides by hostile forces. One by one, Sunni Ali eliminated these threats; the rise of the Songhay empire was due mostly to his victories on the battlefield.

Sunni Ali began by defeating the Mossi, the Dogon, and the Fulani, all formidable warrior groups of the western Sudan. Then he recaptured Timbuktu from the Tuareg raiders of the Sahara, who had seized the city in 1433. Following the course of the Niger River to the west, Sunni Ali then assaulted Jenne, a vital trading center. No attacker had ever been able to take the city, but Sunni Ali patiently besieged it for seven years and captured it in 1476. Eight years after ascending the throne, Sunni Ali had the entire middle Niger region under his control.

Following the pattern of other West African leaders who founded great empires, Sunni Ali was a traditionalist in matters of religion. He was wise enough to pay elaborate respects to the Muslim faith of his trading partners, but he knew that his power rested primarily on the support of the farmers and fishermen of the Niger grasslands; like Sundiata Keita and other founding fathers, he was known primarily as a champion of the old religion. His preference became especially clear in times of crisis. For example, when he recaptured Timbuktu, he confronted the Muslim community with the charge of disloyalty, alleging that they had delivered the city into the hands of the

Tuareg raiders. He then punished the qadis with such severity that the Muslims of Timbuktu thought of him long afterward as a cruel tyrant. But his actions no doubt won the approval of the non-Muslims in the countryside, and experience had clearly taught him that this was the true basis of power in West Africa. Without question, prosperity came from the Muslims of the cities, but the military strength that made peaceful commerce possible depended on the rugged folk of the hinterland, who formed the core of the king's army.

By the time Sunni Ali died in 1492, the Songhay empire surpassed both of its great predecessors, Ghana and Mali. Not only did Sunni Ali conquer and restore order to the Sudan, but he also proved a brilliant administrator. He created provinces where none had existed before, developed new methods of farming, and organized the boatmen of the Niger into the beginnings of a professional navy.

Sunni Ali's son, Sunni Baru, inherited his father's crown but could not recapture the elder man's aura of success. Within a year of taking over the throne, Baru had a serious rebellion on his hands. The root of the problem was his failure to follow his father in bridging the gap between town and country. Rather than paying court both to Islamic traders and practitioners of the old religion, Baru declared that he was a devotee of Songhay's traditional beliefs and that he wanted nothing to do with Islam. Though he correctly understood the basis of his power, he clearly underestimated the risks involved in taking sides so openly.

The Muslims of the towns had endured Sunni Ali's punishments because they had been reassured by his public respect for their religion and his recognition of their importance to the welfare of Songhay. Baru's open hostility, on the other hand, convinced them that they were in danger of losing their influence in the royal court. It would then be only a matter of time before they lost their trading privileges and their wealth. Believing that they now had nothing to lose by rebelling against the king, the Muslims found a leader in Muhammad Turay, a high-ranking army official. Only 14 months into Sunni Baru's reign, Muhammad Turay defeated him in battle and replaced him on the throne.

Muhammad Turay, who became known as Askia Muhammad, ruled from 1493 to 1528. His decision to take the title *askia*, a military rank in the Songhay army, rather than the traditional royal title *sunni*, was an indication of his intention to break with the past. Indeed, his reign brought about a dramatic shift in power from the countryside to the cities, where his support was strongest. Though he did not repeat the error of Sunni Baru by turning his back on a whole segment of Songhay's population, Askia Muhammad's actions made it plain to all that his adherence to Islam was more than a political gesture.

Almost immediately after his victory over Sunni Baru, Askia Muhammad set out on a two-year pilgrimage to Mecca. When he returned home, he began instituting Muslim laws and practices wherever possible, relying on the advice of a North African sage named al-Maghili. By 1500, Leo Africanus, a widely traveled Muslim writer, was able to record the following impression of Timbuktu: "There are many judges, professors, and holy men, all being generously helped by the king, who holds scholars in much honor. Here, too, they sell many handwritten books from North Africa. More profit is made from selling books in Timbuktu than from any other branch of trade."

Askia Muhammad also went further than any previous West African ruler in the organization of his realm. His most important innovation was to open up the ranks of government service. Previously, governors and other leading officials had been appointed on the basis of their birth: they were all heads of

The ancient mosque of Jenne, a major center of Muslim learning during the height of the Songhay empire, looms above an open square.

important clans or descent lines. Askia Muhammad, while honoring the traditional methods, also followed the Muslim principle of equality, which valued learning and piety more than birth. Under Muhammad, able men could achieve high office regardless of their social position.

Askia Muhammad divided his empire into five provinces, each one headed by a governor: Kurmina, Dendi, Baro, Dirma, and Bangu. The central government, based in Gao, consisted of many war chiefs and civil chiefs; most of these chiefs, as in the case of Mali, bore the title *farma*. Askia Muhammad, however, was not content to have a single official in charge of each important governmental function. He also appointed a host of subofficials, creating a structure much like the system of ministers, secretaries, and undersecretaries of modern nations. For example, Songhay's *katisi-farma*, or finance minister, was assisted by the *waney-farma*, who handled all questions of property; the *bara-farma*, who looked after the payment of wages; and the *dey-farma*, who was in charge of all purchasing done by the government. Other departments were divided along similar lines.

Askia Muhammad also took great pains to modernize his military forces, building on the work of Sunni Ali. Previously, the kings of West Africa had relied upon the traditions of feudalism in times of war, calling upon their vassals to provide fighting men. There had been no such thing as a standing army at the command of the king. The advantage of this system was largely economic—the king was spared the expense of housing and feeding a large body of soldiers, and in times of peace the soldiers were free to pursue other occupations. On the other hand, the feudal system caused inevitable delays in gathering and deploying forces. During the 15th and 16th centuries, when African rulers were developing more sophisticated methods of warfare, training and discipline became more important than ever before. A body of amateur soldiers quickly brought together would not have the same prowess in battle as would a group of veterans who enjoyed the benefit of constant training.

Askia Muhammad therefore organized a permanent professional army, under a general who bore the title *dyini-koy*. The king also created a full-time navy made up of Niger boatmen, who served under an admiral known as the *hi-koy*. A third official, the *tara-farma*, was in charge of Songhay's cavalry.

Under Askia Muhammad's administration, the cities of Songhay reached their full flowering. Timbuktu, because of its vulnerability to the Tuareg raiders of the Sahara, never became a leading political center. But, as Leo Africanus noted admiringly, the city was a center of religion and learning, and it produced a number of native-born writers who left valuable records in Arabic of the Songhay empire. One of these writers, Ahmed Baba, created a number of works that—according to Basil Davidson—are still in use among the Muslims of West Africa. Muhammad Kati, born in Timbuktu in 1468, began his great work, *Tarikh al Fattash* (The History of the Seeker of Knowledge), in 1519. As a member of Askia Muhammad's personal staff, Kati accompanied the emperor to Mecca and was thus in a unique position to record the development of Songhay. Reputedly, he lived to the age of 125; his sons and grandsons continued the *Tarikh al Fattash*, bringing the work to completion in 1665.

As in the case of earlier empires, the culture and organization of Songhay depended finally upon the trade that flourished in its cities. In addition to Gao and Timbuktu, the city of Jenne played a significant role in the prosperity of the empire. Located farther west along the Niger, Jenne served as a link between the traders of Timbuktu and the gold producers of the southern forest belt. As Nehemiah Levtzion has pointed out in his book *Ancient Ghana and Mali*, great blocks of salt were transported by canoe from Timbuktu to Jenne, where they were broken up into smaller pieces and carried by porters to the goldfields of the south. Jenne's bustling trade was carried on by the same Mandinka people who had been responsible for the founding of the kingdom of Mali: they had centered their operations in Jenne since the decline of the Mali empire. The city itself, protected by its location in the flood plain of the Niger and by a high defensive wall, had never been under the control of Mali; it had remained independent until it was taken by Sunni Ali in the 1470s. During the 17th century, the scholar al-Sa'di described the city in terms that certainly would have applied during the heyday of Songhay: "This city is large, flourishing, and prosperous. . . . Jenne is one of the great markets of the Muslim world. There one meets the salt merchants from the mines of Teghaza and merchants carrying gold from the mines of Bitou. . . . Because of this blessed city,

This terra-cotta sculpture, found during excavations near Jenne, may have been produced as early as the 1300s. The snake on the figure's forehead suggests its connection with the Niger belt's traditional religions, which have deep ties to the animal world.

caravans flock to Timbuktu from all points of the horizon. . . . The area around Jenne is fertile and well populated; with numerous markets held there on all the days of the week. It is certain that it contains 7,077 villages very near to one another."

Though Jenne was a flourishing Muslim center in the Songhay empire and continues to function today in the republic of Mali, with its ancient mosque still in use, archaeologists have concluded from examining ancient burial sites that the city was originally founded by non-Islamic Africans who observed the traditional religions. It appears that the city owed its initial rise—at least as early as A.D. 1000—to the fertility of the Niger flood plain, which made it possible for the inhabitants to produce a surplus of rice and other grains, which they could then trade to less productive communities. Thus, Graham Connah concluded in *African Civilizations* that "it seems most likely that an extensive trading network existed within West Africa before the Arab trade across the Sahara was developed. The savanna towns were indeed 'ports' at the edge of the 'sea of land' . . . but they were ports with a vast trading hinterland that was already developed. After all, what ship would ever visit a port unless there was a chance of a cargo to collect?" Archaeologists' findings confirm once again that no one group or culture was responsible for the success of West Africa; the region's growth was the result of the rich ferment of many different traditions.

That ferment had long before shown its tendency to tear down the very empires it had helped build up. Less than 40 years after the death of Askia Muhammad, his careful work began to come undone. During the reign of Askia Muhammad II (1582–86), the Hausa states in the east rose up against the rule of

The great emperor Askia Muhammad was buried in this tomb at Gao, the seat of the Songhay government.

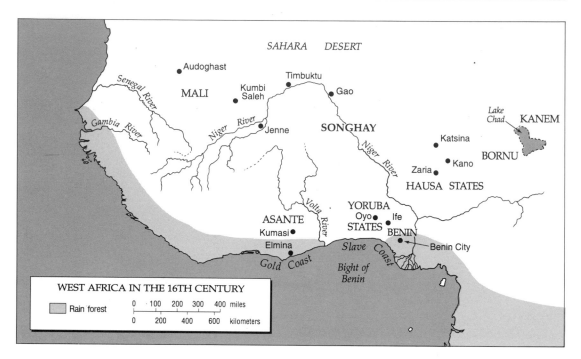

WEST AFRICA IN THE 16TH CENTURY

From the 1460s to the end of the next century, Songhay's rulers dominated the Western Sudan. This map indicates both the breadth of their empire and the diversity of their West African rivals.

Songhay, and the Moroccans of North Africa seized the salt deposits at Teghaza, in the northern reaches of the empire. The latter event led to a full-scale war between Morocco and Songhay.

The Moroccans were a formidable enemy. In 1578, they had successfully defended their territory against an invading force from the European nation of Portugal, annihilating the Portuguese king Sebastian and almost 25,000 of his soldiers at the Battle of Alcazarquivir. (By this victory, they delayed the European penetration of Africa by more than two centuries.) Then, in 1590, Morocco's sultan Mulay Ahmad, known as Mulay the Victorious, sent a 4,600-man army south through the Sahara to capture the riches of Songhay. Such a small force should not have stood much chance against the armies of Songhay, but the Moroccans had two important factors weighing in their favor. First, at least half of them were equipped with harquebuses. The harquebus, a European invention, was an early form of musket, and as such provided its users with a tremendous advantage over opponents armed with swords, spears, and bows and arrows. Second, many of the Moroccan troops were Spanish and Portuguese Christians who had been taken prisoner in warfare or captured by Muslim pirates. Their lives had been spared on condition that they become Muslims and fight for the sultan. Though they had no personal loyalty to Mulay, they certainly knew that retreat would mean either death in the Sahara or execution when they returned to Morocco, and they fought with the ferocity of desperate men.

The first battle between Morocco and Songhay, which took place at Tondibi in March 1591, resulted in a clear-cut victory for the invaders. Fighting their way steadily southward, they penetrated both Gao and Timbuktu and carried off much gold and other valuable goods. The armies of Songhay's Ishaq II proved incapable of driving the Moroccans back across the desert, but the country people did what they could to harass the invaders. The scholar al-Sa'di provided a vivid account of the chaos caused by the Moroccans: "This expeditionary force found the Sudan one of God's most favored countries in prosperity, comfort, security, and vitality. . . . Then all that changed; security gave place to danger, prosperity made way for misery and calamity, whilst affliction and distress succeeded well being. Over the length and breadth of the land people began to devour one another, raids and war spared neither life nor wealth. Disorder spread and intensified until it became universal."

As the disorder prevented the towns from providing riches to the crown and the empire of Songhay lost its splendid possessions, the country people—the true foundation of Songhay's power—once again became the backbone of the nation. In the rise and fall of Songhay, history seemed to have come full circle.

5

THE LAKE PEOPLE

✳

IN the entire western Sudan, there is only one sizable body of water—Lake Chad. The lake, which can cover an area as large as 9,000 square miles in periods of adequate rainfall, is situated on the border of the present-day nations of Chad, Niger, and Nigeria. As early as the beginning of the Iron Age, Lake Chad was a natural point of settlement along the trade routes leading into West Africa, both from the Sahara and from Egypt. Thus the people who lived in the region were in touch with much of the rest of Africa.

Around 850, the Kanuri people founded the state of Kanem in the vicinity of Lake Chad. The exact origin of the Kanuri is unknown, but there is reason to believe that they were made up in part of migrants from the Nile valley who brought a somewhat different racial and cultural strain into the Sudan. These migrants, known as the Sao, no longer exist as a distinct people, but archaeologists have uncovered intriguing evidence of their civilization. "With the

This wooden board from Hausaland, in what is now northern Nigeria, is inscribed with Arabic text from the Koran. Such boards were used as writing tablets in the region's Islamic schools.

A 19th-century engraving shows cattle visiting a watering hole near Lake Chad, the largest body of water in the western Sudan. The roofs of a village can be seen in the background.

appearance of the Sao in the neighborhood of Lake Chad," Basil Davidson has written, "there is both an end to the civilizing trail which had led from the valley of the Nile and the beginning of another civilization. For the Sao constructed towns, fashioned rams' heads in pottery, worked in bronze . . . , elevated women to influence in government, and generally elaborated a mode of life that was plainly a new synthesis of the African east and African west."

The Kanuris' new state was governed by kings belonging to the Sefawa dynasty, and by the 12th century, these kings eventually followed many of their fellow rulers in adopting Islam. The act of reaching out to the Muslim trading powers of the north and east remained an almost certain formula for prosperity, expansion, and influence.

By the reign of Dunama Dibbelimi (1221–59), the
state of Kanem had grown into an empire. Kanem's
original boundaries had expanded around Lake Chad
and hundreds of miles to the north, absorbing trade
routes that extended to the borders of North Africa.
Kanem maintained this position for more than a century, until it came under assault from the Bulala, a
neighboring people to the east. By the end of the 14th
century, Kanem had lost its territory east of the lake,
including its capital city, Nkimi. The reigning Sefawa
king, Umar, then established a new capital at Bornu.
For this reason, the Sefawa empire has usually been
known to historians as Kanem-Bornu.

Having retreated at first, the rulers of Kanem-
Bornu gathered their strength and resumed the offen-
sive. During the 15th century, Kanem-Bornu regained
many of its former possessions and also made major
inroads to the west, in the territory of the Hausa
people. However, the greatest era of the empire did
not begin until the reign of Idris Alooma, which
extended from 1580 until 1617 (some historians have
suggested the alternate dates of 1571–1603).

Like Askia Muhammad of Songhay and other
previous empire builders, Idris believed that the future
of his people lay in the path of Islam. He took measures to promote the influence of Islamic law, even
going so far as to submit his own affairs to the judgment of the Muslim qadis.

**Idris Alooma led Kanem-Bornu to its highest
level of influence. By the time he was done, his
empire extended far beyond the boundaries of the
original Kanem: it reached all the way to Murzuk
in the northern Sahara and far beyond Lake
Chad to the hills of Darfur in the east. As the
ruler of this domain, Idris was so powerful that**

he received ambassadors from the Ottoman Empire, which had spread from Turkey throughout the Middle East and was then in control of Cairo, Egypt. Idris's rule roughly coincided with that of England's Elizabeth I; though much less has been written about him, he was no less successful or grand a monarch.

In addition to the king, Kanem-Bornu was run by a council of governors, perhaps a dozen in number. The governors were all members of the ruling Sefawa family, and each of them presided over a province of the empire. Because of the rebelliousness of neighboring peoples, especially those in the east, the borders of Kanem-Bornu were constantly shifting. But the king and the governors were able to maintain enough stability that trade went on without serious disruption. From the north and east came Arabian horses, fine metalware, salt, and copper; from Kanem-Bornu, kola nuts, gold, and ivory reached the outside world.

After the death of Idris, peace and prosperity reigned for another century—under the kings Muhammad, Ibrahim, and Omar—even though much of the Sudan was in turmoil because of the decline of Mali and Songhay. The tide of history did not even begin to overtake Kanem-Bornu until the end of the 17th century, when raiders from both north and south pressed in on the empire. The Sefawa carried on despite their shrinking borders. The last representative of their line, Ahmad, held the throne until 1846, when he was ousted by the Fulani leader Uthman Dan Fodio. Thus the Sefawa had enjoyed an unbroken reign from the 9th century into the 19th, a record of stability and prosperity rarely equaled in human history.

Throughout its history, Kanem-Bornu had been in close contact—sometimes peaceful, sometimes violent—with the Hausa states, located directly west of Kanem in what is now northern Nigeria. The main Hausa states—Biram, Daura, Gobir, Kano, Katsina, Rano, and Zaria—had a royal tradition nearly as old as Kanem's, and in many ways they resembled the fiefs of medieval Europe. Each of the Hausa states was ruled by its own king, and for as long as they had existed they had competed with one another for wealth and power in the region. The life of each centered on a fortified city in which the people of the countryside would take shelter in times of war or other crises. As in Europe, the country people paid a tax to the local leader (*sarki*) in the form of goods or money. The sarkis were subservient to the king, to whom they paid a tax of their own. In addition to offering protection, the cities provided markets for the produce of the countryside and served as an outlet for visiting traders.

Much current knowledge about the Hausa states derives from the *Kano Chronicle*, a collection of oral accounts that were written down long after the events they described. The chronicle makes it clear that the Hausa kings faced the same challenge as other West African rulers: they had to balance the political and religious needs of the cities against those of the countryside. For example, the chronicle relates that a 13th-century sarki named Shekkaru was advised by his counselors to send troops to fight against country people who were showing signs of disloyalty. The counselors argued, as many have before and since, that if Shekkaru tried to negotiate with the people, they would consider him weak. Shekkaru, however, believed that bloodshed should always be a last resort. (Fighting, after all, disrupted trade.) He received a delegation of rural chiefs who were also eager to avoid a violent clash. "If the lands of a ruler are wide, he should be patient," they told the sarki. "But if his lands are not wide, he will certainly not be able to gain

This offering bowl, a product of the Yoruba tribe, was made to hold kola nuts—bitter, caffeine-containing seeds valued throughout West Africa for their stimulant properties.

possession of the whole countryside by impatience." Shekkaru understood the wisdom of their words and decided to work with them rather than try to conquer them.

As the centuries unfolded, none of the Hausa kings was able to acquire truly "wide lands" by bringing all of the Hausa states under his rule. On the whole, the Hausa cooperated more than they fought, largely because they had an important role in the economy of West Africa. Situated closer than any other savanna state to the Niger delta and the forestlands of the coast, the Hausa states were in close contact with the Yoruba people, who harvested kola nuts (valued for their stimulant properties); in turn, the Yoruba could only get the outside goods they needed through Hausaland.

As a result of this trade, the Hausa cities grew to be as prosperous and cultured as any in the Sudan. They were protected by soldiers whose elaborate suits of armor were famous for their strength and splendor. Leo Africanus, traveling in the area during the 17th century, noted the wealth of the rulers and the size of their armies and was especially impressed by the state of Kano, which was rich in corn, rice, and cotton: "Also here are many deserts and wild, woody mountains containing many springs of water. In these woods grow plenty of wild citrons and lemons, which differ not much in taste from the best of all. In the midst of this province stands a town of the same name, the walls and houses whereof are built for the most part of a kind of chalk [the typical clay of West Africa]. The inhabitants are rich merchants and most civil people."

Prosperity had its price. Taxes in the Hausa states were high, and Leo Africanus also noted on his travels that people outside the cities lived poorly: during the winter, they had nothing but animal skins to cover themselves with, and during the summer, they went all but naked. The Hausa kings had also developed an extensive system of slave labor. The slaves were obtained from neighboring states during military raids. Abdullah Burja, a 15th-century ruler of Kano, was said to command more than 20,000 slaves in a number of settlements. Some of these slaves were recruited into full-time armies; the military establishments originated by Askia Muhammad of Songhay were now common throughout the Sudan.

In addition to the burden they imposed on the countryside, the Hausa cities were wealthy enough to be seen as a rich prize by potential conquerors.

Traders enter the city of Kano, Nigeria, one of the most prosperous Hausa centers of commerce.

("It is the hen with chickens that fears the hawk," runs a Hausa proverb.) Askia Muhammad himself conquered Kano during the 16th century and compelled its ruler to pay him one-third of the city's revenue. Following Kano's submission, Zaria became the strongest of the Hausa states. Zaria is noteworthy because its rise was due in large part to the efforts of female rulers, Barkwa Turunda and her daughter, Queen Amina, who conquered a number of neighboring states and undertook many building projects in their domains. Eventually, the states subdued by Zaria, notably Jukun, turned the tables on their conquerors and enjoyed their own periods of dominance. But the wars between the rival states do not appear to have been especially long or destructive, because the general prosperity of Hausaland continued. In fact, the 16th century represented a peak of achievement for Hausaland and for neighboring areas of the Sudan.

Like many of the nations of Europe, West Africans were by this time moving away from a long-held idea: that the king was not a high-ranking public figure, but a higher form of being. According to Nehemiah Levtzion, this idea may have reached its absolute peak in Kanem in earlier times; in his discussion of the subject, he quotes the testimony of al-Muhallabi, a Muslim scholar who visited Kanem during the 10th century: "They exalt their king and worship him instead of God. They imagine that he does not eat. . . . If any of his subjects meet the camels which carry the food [secretly to his palace] he is instantly killed. . . . Their religion is the worship of their kings, for they believe that they bring life and death, sickness and health."

In the place of divine kingship, West Africans gradually developed the idea of constitutional monarchy, in which the king's power was limited by carefully drawn political rules. By the 18th century, the Hausa kings were able to take action on important issues only with the consent of senior advisers. In addition to counselors who were heads of major descent lines, the rulers also surrounded themselves with individuals known as king's men. Many of the king's men were eunuchs, men who had been castrated so that they could not begin descent lines of their own; thus their only loyalty would be to the king. In many cases, the king's men came into conflict with the advisers who had been appointed because of their birth; when this happened, skillful rulers could play off one faction against another and gain leverage in making decisions.

Even though they achieved a high level of political development, the Hausa states never combined to form a powerful empire, even after the decline of Kanem-Bornu. The Hausa kings were simply unable to abandon their rivalries, and they wasted much energy and valuable resources in fighting one another. By the mid-18th century, the westernmost states were repeatedly ravaged by Tuareg raiders from the Sahara. And by the beginning of the following century, the Hausa kings faced a full-scale revolt from within—far more dangerous than any external threat.

The rebellion was not a simple grab for power but rather a reform movement within the Islamic community, to which all the rulers belonged. The movement arose among the Fulani, who had played an important role throughout the history of the Sudan, and it was led by Uthman Dan Fodio. Though he was a member of the Quadiriyya, a Muslim brotherhood that was soon to be considered conservative, Uthman adopted a radical stance. He denounced the luxury of the Hausa cities and called for substantial reforms in the way the states were governed. His message was designed to rally the support of the humble country people, Muslim and non-Muslim alike, who readily agreed with Uthman's words condemning "the collecting of concubines and fine clothes and horses that run in the towns, not on the battlefields, and the devouring of gifts of influence, booty, and bribery."

Uthman and his followers deposed the Hausa kings one by one. But they did not find it easy to achieve their cherished goal of the ideal Islamic state that would carry out all the dictates of the Koran. Disputes arose among the Fulani leaders, and these were not resolved until Sultan Muhammad Bello, Uthman's son, imposed his will upon the Fulani by force of arms. By that measure, however, the democratic element of the reform movement was destroyed. Thus the Hausa states finally achieved unity under Muhammad Bello, but they also lost the political qualities that had made them unique. By the early 20th century, the Hausa had a new set of masters, the colonial governors of the British Empire, who also took control of the former territory of Kanem-Bornu around Lake Chad. Today, the Islamic culture that blossomed in these regions survives in the northern part of Nigeria, Africa's most populous republic.

6

THE FORESTLANDS

THE doom and ironwood trees were frequent; the path was a labyrinth of the most capricious windings, the roots of the cotton trees obstructing it continually, and our progress was generally by stepping and jumping up and down, rather than walking. . . . Immense trunks of fallen trees presented constant barriers to our progress, and increased our fatigues from the labor of scaling them. . . . The large trees were covered with parasites and convulvuli, and the climbing plants, like small cables, ascending the trunks to some height, abruptly shot downwards, crossed to the opposite trees, and threaded each other in such a perplexity of twists and turnings, that it soon became impossible to trace them in the general entanglement." Such was the experience of a 19th-century European, quoted by Graham Connah, in the tropical rain forest of the West African coast. Protected since the Stone Age by this dense and forbidding landscape, the peoples of the forest enjoyed a way of life strikingly different from that of the inhabitants of the savanna.

Between the 10th and 16th centuries, Yoruba artists in the city of Ife created bronze and terra-cotta portraits of exceptional strength and beauty. The elegance of this bronze cast is characteristic of the Ife legacy.

A man from the modern state of Guinea crosses a narrow bridge in the West African rain forest.

The Igbo, for example, who occupied a large area just east of the Niger River, had neither kings nor chiefs. Living in forest villages and skilled in farming, they practiced what is known as segmentary government. The basis of segmentary government is the family unit. As a family grows and new generations begin their own branches, new segments break off from the original line and form a distinct unit in a nearby area.

At first glance, this way of life might appear to cause disunity and weakness. However, the Igbo religion included many ceremonies designed to strengthen family and community ties. Some of these ceremonies emphasized the importance of a family's common ancestors; others formally transferred power from older segments of a family to newer segments, thus reminding all parties of their rights and responsibilities.

Throughout Igboland, different groups developed their own responses to situations calling for mutual aid. Some groups, such as the Ama and Ozo, formed associations that were governed by the wealthiest members; others, such as the Tallensi, insisted on strict equality in decision making. Compared to the centralized states and empires of the savanna, with their elaborate rituals of kingship and luxurious royal courts, the Igbo maintained a remarkably democratic way of life that was much closer in spirit to the 19th and 20th centuries than to the Middle Ages.

A neighboring people who enjoyed an equally distinctive way of life was the Yoruba. Living to the west of the Niger, the Yoruba traced their roots to the very dawn of civilization. According to one of their traditions, both the Yoruba nation and humanity itself were created at the town of Ile-Ife.

In one version of the Yoruba creation story, the world was created by the Supreme Being, Olodumare, through his agent Orishanla, who then brought human beings out of the sky to dwell on the earth. But according to a parallel belief, the world was created by the god Odududwa, who came not from the sky but from the east: he brought the Yoruba with him to the land of the Niger and then sired rulers for various communities. As Basil Davidson has interpreted the two traditions, they do not really conflict but rather supplement one another: "What right could any peo-

The Igbo religion, like many other African faiths, involved many practices that strengthened family and community ties. This female figure comes from an Igbo shrine devoted to family ancestors.

ple have to come from somewhere else and settle in a new land? . . . To seal their right to occupy and settle, incomers must make their peace with the Spirit of the Earth. They could do this only through a process of spiritual reconciliation sanctioned by appropriate rites. Otherwise the Spirit of the Earth would not recognize their legitimate existence in the land."

Archaeologists have confirmed that the ancestors of the Yoruba came to the West African forestland from the central Sudan (not the east, as the tradition claims) sometime after A.D. 700, blending with peoples who had occupied the Niger region since the Stone Age. The older inhabitants were already skilled in iron making and may have been related to the brilliantly creative Nok culture. The newcomers, though less adept as craftspeople, brought a new level of political sophistication.

Because of this influx of political ideas, the new Yoruba communities developed quite differently from those of the Igbo. Though the Yoruba practiced the same farming techniques in the dense forests, they did not limit the size of their settlements as the Igbo did. The Yoruba built a number of large towns, most of which were surrounded by sizable walls. Each town was ruled by an *oba*, who was said to be descended from Odududwa, the god who had brought the Yoruba into the forestland.

Yoruba towns did resemble Igbo villages in their general structure: they were organized on segmentary lines, with each family group occupying its own distinct area. All the dwellings belonging to a family were clustered together in a compound known as an *agbo'le*. At the center of this compound was the house of the head of the descent line to which all the various offshoots belonged. Following the same idea, the agbo'les were clustered around the house of the oba, which stood in the center of the town.

The oba was generally chosen by a council of

The tradition that produced this terra-cotta head from Ife drew inspiration from the Nok culture, a civilization that may have preceded the Yoruba empire by as much as a thousand years.

chiefs. But when major decisions had to be made, the Yoruba did not practice the village democracy of the Igbo. On the contrary, the oba alone held the power to take action, aided by his personal servants and messengers, who formed a class comparable to the officialdom of the savanna kingdoms. For truly large-scale decision making, the various obas and their

This richly ornamented Ife half-figure is believed to represent an oni, *the highest authority in the Ebi system of government.*

towns were linked through the Yoruba's Ebi system of government. In the Ebi system, each town had the status of a descent line: all were united as equals in the great "family" of the Yoruba people, under the guidance of a supreme authority, the *oni* of Ife.

Ife reached its peak during the 14th century. As a

civilization, it is remembered not so much for its political majesty as for the brilliance of its craftspeople and artists. Beginning as early as the 10th century, its sculptors and metalworkers produced works of art that were a direct outgrowth of the Nok culture. Fashioned both in terra-cotta and in bronze, the sculptures are predominantly portrayals of human heads. Their combination of realistic detail, abstract design, and spiritual intensity places them among the world's greatest works of art. Indeed, the rest of the world spent many centuries catching up with Ife: many of the pioneers of modern art in Europe, such as the great Spanish painter Pablo Picasso, acknowledged the influence of African art on their seemingly revolutionary works.

Ife's accomplishments ensured that it would remain the spiritual center of the Yoruba nation. But by the 16th century, Ife and all the other Yoruba communities were gradually overshadowed by the town of Oyo. Situated in the northern part of the forest belt, Oyo—one of the newer towns—was in an ideal position to benefit from trading opportunities with the savanna states.

Before it could truly take the lead in Yorubaland, Oyo had to solve the problem of self-defense. Throughout its history, the town had been victimized by two of the Hausa states, Nupe and Borgu, both of which possessed powerful mounted armies. Oyo's *alafin* (king) Orompoto resolved to build up his forces to match those of his enemies, but to do so he had to overcome a serious obstacle. Oyo was situated in a region inhabited by the tsetse fly, one of Africa's most dangerous pests. The bloodsucking tsetse not only threatens humans with a variety of diseases, such as sleeping sickness; it also transmits a fatal ailment, known as nagana, to cattle and horses. For this reason, it was impossible for the people of Oyo to breed their own horses. But under Orompoto they discovered that horses imported from North Africa could survive the tsetse long enough to be serviceable. Fortunately, the people of Oyo were wealthy enough to purchase a steady supply of mounts from the north. Orompoto trained a crack force of 1,000 cavalry, and Oyo no longer had any problems with its neighbors.

Its security assured, Oyo set about building an empire. In addition to its favorable geographic position, Oyo had much to offer traders. The Yoruba excelled in the art of making fine cotton goods, and their textiles were in great demand throughout Africa, Asia, and Europe. They continued to produce world-class metalwork, as well as first-rate bowls and jugs. The more income these products brought them, the better the Yoruba were able to maintain their formidable cavalry.

From the 16th through the 18th centuries, the combination of commercial and military power allowed Oyo to spread its influence both into the savanna and deeper into the forestlands. Oyo's most important conquest was the state of Dahomey: this acquisition placed Oyo in control of a seaport, Porto-Novo on the Gulf of Guinea, from which the Yoruba were able to deal with the European merchants now plying the coast. As they became ever more powerful as traders and warriors, the alafins of Oyo assumed almost superhuman dimensions in the eyes of their subjects. According to Basil Davidson, the people of Dahomey told an English visitor "that when the Oyo people want to go to war, their general 'spreads the hide of a buffalo before the door of his tent and pitches a spear in the ground on each side of it. Between these spears the soldiers march until the multitude which pass over the hide have worn a hole in it. As soon as this happens, the general presumes that his forces are numerous enough to take the field.'"

By the end of the 18th century, Oyo was said to control as many as 6,600 towns and villages. However, the alafins became so intent on trading that they began to neglect their army, which was ultimately the basis of their power in the region. In addition, their method of rule was ill-suited to the task of governing a large empire. In theory, Oyo had a perfectly workable method of controlling conquered territories: a Yoruba chief lived in the capital city of each subject state and ran its affairs, much in the manner of the European colonial governors who were later to make their appearance in Africa. As the empire grew, however, the alafins of Oyo found it increasingly difficult to keep in touch with their governors. The difficulty sprang from the very nature of their society. Like most of the forest peoples, the Yoruba had never deviated in any way from their ancestral religions; even the rulers had not felt the need to curry favor with Muslim traders by converting to Islam. The old ways satisfied all the Yoruba's social, spiritual, and artistic needs but did not provide them with one tool that had proved highly useful to the rulers of the Sudan: the art of reading and writing.

As their society grew, the Yoruba had clearly not been hampered by their lack of literacy. Indeed, if they had developed a literary tradition, they might never have felt the need to express themselves in the magnificent art of Ife. But once Oyo moved away from the Ebi style of family-oriented government and began to emulate the far-flung empires of the savanna, the illiteracy of alafins and governors became a severe handicap. The alafins could not issue any written instructions to their public servants. They had to rely on their messengers to memorize verbal commands and deliver them accurately after traveling long distances: the potential for mistakes and treachery in this method was clearly unlimited.

Subject states and rivals were eager to assert themselves against the power of the alafins, and they watched them for signs of weakness. The situation was

The rulers of Oyo never converted to Islam but remained true to the traditional religions of the African forestlands. Oyo leaders used this brass rattle to call on ancestral spirits.

further complicated by tensions within the Yoruba community, as the nobles of other towns often resented Oyo's departure from the Ebi tradition of equality. In addition, Oyo's increasing trade in slaves and firearms was creating unstable conditions along the coast.

Before long, the smaller states on the coast took advantage of Oyo's state of confusion and tried to seize control of the trade routes in their territory, disrupting Oyo's economy. Roland Oliver and Anthony Atmore have recounted the course of events in *Africa Since 1800*:

> The beginning of the end came in 1817, when the great chiefs of Oyo, led by Alfonja of Ilorin, sent an empty calabash [a gourd used as a bottle or dipper] to the *alafin* (king) Aole, thus signifying that they no longer recognized his authority. Aole accepted the hint in traditional fashion by committing suicide, but not before he had uttered his famous curse. From the palace forecourt he shot three arrows, one to the north, one to the south, and one to the west, saying, "My curse be on you for your disloyalty and disobedience, so let your children disobey you. If you send them on an errand, let them never return to bring you word again. To all the points I shot my arrows will you be carried as slaves. My curse will carry you to the sea and beyond the seas, slaves will rule over you, and you, their masters, will become slaves."

Forming another threat from the coast, the people of Dahomey were growing strong enough to cause problems for Oyo's military forces. And the Fulani, who had taken control of the Hausa states, began to expand under the rule of Muhammad Bello, swooping down on the northern Oyo towns. By about 1840, the power of Oyo had been broken for all time.

Oyo may have vanished into the mists of history, but the civilization of the Yoruba lived on through the trials of slavery and colonialism. Today, the 10 million Yoruba of Nigeria form the nation's third-largest ethnic group. As the Yoruba continue to practice their traditional occupations, such as farming and cotton weaving, their ancient city-dwelling traditions remain intact: Nigeria's 10 largest cities are predominantly Yoruba. Moreover, Olodumare and the other Yoruba gods are powerfully alive, not only in Africa but also in the Americas—particularly in Brazil and Cuba— where many Yoruba were transported as slaves during the 18th and 19th centuries. The harmony and depth of the Yoruba worldview has exerted widespread appeal even among non-Africans, and the ancient art inspired by these beliefs remains one of the treasures of world culture.

7

GRANDEUR IN THE DELTA

W HILE the Yoruba were developing their network of great towns in the forestland, another
ancient people, the Edo, were establishing themselves
in the Niger delta, the region where the great river
forms several branches before it flows into the Gulf of
Guinea. The Edo's traditions show that they were in
close contact with the Yoruba: they trace the beginnings of what was to become the powerful empire
of Benin to Prince Oranmiyan, a son of the Yoruba
god Odududwa.

Despite this time-honored connection, neither
the Edo nor Benin was ever dominated by the Yoruba
states. The Edo's position in the Niger delta, along the
main travel route between the sea and the inland
regions, gave them rich opportunities for trade. By the
14th century, Benin was a rising commercial power;
by the 15th century, it was a mighty empire. Ewuare,
the Edo *oba* (king) who led the way to expansion,
ascended the throne around 1440. Ewuare is credited

*This 17th-century bronze plaque from Benin depicts members of
the oba's court. The figure on the left is holding a sistrum—a
kind of rattle used by the musicians of the ancient Near East.*

by Edo tradition with conquering more than 200 towns and villages and with developing Benin City, which became the capital of the empire.

A century or so later, a Dutch traveler named Olfert Dapper found the city highly impressive:

> At the gate where I went in on horseback, I saw a very big wall, very thick and made of earth, with a very deep and broad ditch outside it. . . . Inside the gate, and along the great street just mentioned, you see many other great streets on either side, and these are also straight and do not bend. . . . The houses in this town stand in good order, each one close and evenly placed with its neighbor, just as the houses in Holland stand. . . . The king's court is very great. It is built around many square-shaped yards. These yards have surrounding galleries where sentries are always placed. I myself went into the court far enough to pass through four great yards like this, and yet wherever I looked I could still see gate after gate which opened into other yards.

Oba Ewuare and his 16th-century successor Oba Esigie were equally famed for their innovations in government. Ewuare founded the State Council of Benin to govern the growing empire, and Esigie developed a civil service, recruiting officials on the basis of ability rather than social position.

Laying the ground for the later history of West Africa, these kings developed large-scale trade relations with Europeans. By the 15th and 16th centuries, Europe had recovered from the ravages of war and plague and was entering an era of expansion. At the forefront of the expansionist movement was the nation of Portugal, situated on the Atlantic coast of the Iberian Peninsula. Portugal, a narrow kingdom with a long coastline, became a nation of seafarers, and Portuguese ships had been sailing to North Africa since the beginning of the 14th century. However, Portuguese sailors were for many years unable to pass beyond Cape Bojador in the northwest because of the

This richly detailed Benin sculpture represents a Portuguese soldier brandishing a matchlock. Arriving in Benin in 1472, the Portuguese left a deep impression on the lives of the Edo, giving them direct access to European weapons and other manufactured goods.

prevailing north-to-south winds: a ship that sailed down the western coast of Africa could not return. With the invention of the lateen (triangular) sail and the sternpost rudder, however, ships could finally sail into the wind; and when the Portuguese added these features to the newly designed caravel, a smaller and more maneuverable ship, they had nothing to fear from the winds south of Bojador. In 1472, Portuguese sailors dropped anchor in the Bight of Benin, a wide bay in the Gulf of Guinea, and made contact with the wealthy rulers of the Edo's growing empire.

At first, relations between the two continents benefited both Europeans and Africans. The Africans were able to purchase manufactured goods and metals such as copper from the Europeans instead of sending all the way to North Africa; they were also able to sell their gold, ivory, and spices directly to the Europeans without the use of middlemen. As a result of their contact with Europeans, the rulers of Benin adopted arts and interests that were not usually found in the forest belt. Oba Esigie, who came to power in 1504 and reigned for nearly 50 years, was said, for example, to be able both to speak and to read Portuguese. He also became adept in the art of astrology, the study of the influence of the stars and planets upon human affairs.

During Esigie's reign, English ships made their first contact with Benin, landing at the river port of Gwato, and the British were soon followed by their Dutch rivals. Esigie quickly established a monopoly on the new source of trade. According to one Dutch traveler, "Nobody is allowed to buy anything from the Europeans on this coast, except the agents and merchants whom the king has named for this purpose. As soon as one of our ships drops anchor, the people inform the king, and the king appoints two or three agents and thirty or forty merchants whom he empowers to deal with the Europeans."

In the ensuing decades, however, the commerce between Europeans and West Africans took a more sinister turn. The change was brought about by the European conquest of the New World. As the European nations—Spain in particular—developed sizable

Heads of Portuguese traders surmount this ornamental ivory mask, made to be worn at the waist of an oba's costume.

colonies in the Americas, they created farming and mining operations that called for vast amounts of human labor. This demand could be met neither by the home countries nor by the native Indian populations of the Americas. The home countries were too small, and the Indians were unaccustomed to the kind of work required by their conquerors; when forced into it, they simply sickened and died. West Africans, on the other hand, were strong and hardy, and they had a long history of tropical farming and metal mining. Determined to make their New World enterprises profitable, the Europeans decided to solve their problem by importing labor from West Africa.

West Africa itself had no tradition of paid labor. Those Africans who did not live independently as farmers were usually organized into various forms of forced labor by African rulers. The wealth of the great empires had always rested upon the exploitation of the weak by the strong, an experience hardly limited to Africa. The Roman Empire; the great civilizations of Egypt, Persia, and Babylon; the Muslim caliphates of the Middle East and North Africa—all had taken slavery as a matter of course. Empires were built and solidified in no small part by the conquest of neighboring nations; as a result of those conquests, subject peoples were obliged—in addition to military service—to produce wealth for their new masters. All the great African leaders, from Mansa Musa to Askia Muhammad, had commanded vast numbers of slaves in their far-flung dominions as well as in their personal entourages. Europeans themselves had continued to enslave each other even as they entered the supposedly enlightened period known as the Renaissance; Italy's Venetian Republic, for example, did a brisk business during the 15th and 16th centuries by exporting Christian slaves from Europe to Muslim North Africa.

Because slavery was already a fact of life in West Africa, it was natural that a small-scale traffic in slaves began as soon as commercial contact was established with Europeans. In the beginning, the Portuguese

were willing to accept a certain number of slaves in exchange for their manufactured goods. But as the demand for slaves in the Americas exploded during the 17th century, the trade in human beings began to dominate the commercial relations between Europe and West Africa. At this point, West African rulers were increasingly in need of European firearms in order to maintain their power. The only way they could obtain these weapons was to provide large numbers of captives for the slave ships. Before long, rulers were going to war against their neighbors not to expand their territory but simply to take prisoners who could then be sold to the Europeans. In order to fight

Elmina Castle, built by the Portuguese in what is now Ghana, became the center of Dutch slave-trading activities in 1637. Pictured here is a courtyard of the female slave quarters, where women captured by the armies of West African rulers awaited shipment to the Americas.

This Igbo dance headdress shows a slave trader bringing a captive woman into European headquarters along the West African coast. By the 18th century, the slave trade had become one of the area's main industries.

these wars, they needed more firearms. And in order to obtain more firearms, they needed to supply more slaves. Thus West Africa was plunged into a vicious cycle that caused untold suffering and ultimately benefited no one but the slave traders.

The transatlantic slave trade not only corrupted the political life of West Africa; it also added a new level of injustice to the institution of slavery as Africans had known it. As Basil Davidson has pointed out, slaves in West African society had a far different position from those sent abroad: "These 'wageless workers' . . . were seldom or never mere chattels, persons without rights or hope of emancipation. . . . They were not . . . outcasts in the body politic. On the contrary, they were integral members of their community. Household slaves lived with their masters, often as members of the family. They could work themselves free of their obligations. They could marry their masters' daughters. They could become traders, leading men in peace and war, governors or sometimes even kings." No such possibilities lay in wait for Africans shipped to the Americas, where they suffered both the hardships of forced labor in a strange land and the added injury of being despised because of their race.

Though historians do not agree on the degree to which the massive slave trade disrupted the economic development of Africa, the effects were certainly significant. A number of areas were quickly depopulated of strong, hardworking men and women who produced both food and such handicrafts as the fine cottons for which Africa had been famous. Though the population in these regions eventually returned to its previous levels, the economy of West Africa suffered long-term damage. Africans who had once exported goods now had to import them, and the price of those imports was tallied in human lives.

The slave trade also upset the age-old political balance of West Africa. Subject peoples could no longer expect, in the natural course of events, to turn the tables on their conquerors and eventually begin their own empires. In the rising tide of violence and exploitation, which even the most enlightened rulers could not escape, Africans became more and more dependent on Europeans for their well-being and their political survival.

Benin was one of the states that suffered most from this corruption of the West African way of life. The inhabitants of Benin City continued to impress Europeans with their elegant dress and manners, but as the slave trade gained momentum, the obas began to lose their power. Firearms spread throughout the region at an uncontrollable pace, and the more these weapons got into the hands of Benin's rivals, the more chance there was of rebellion and attack by competing powers. Increasingly, the governors of outlying areas asserted their own power in defiance of the obas. Benin's empire shrank steadily in power and prestige until it was overwhelmed by British forces in 1897. All that remains of the great delta empire today is Benin City itself, a community of 160,000 in southern Nigeria. (The modern-day nation of Benin, formerly the French colony of Dahomey, is completely distinct from the vanished realm of the obas.)

For all the wealth and influence of its great days, Benin is remembered most of all for its brilliant works of art. The Europeans who plundered Benin in the late 19th and early 20th centuries were astonished by the beauty of the bronze plaques they discovered in the royal palace. Having convinced themselves that the people they were conquering represented a lower form of civilization, the colonialists could not believe that such works had been produced by "savage" Africans. Basil Davidson describes this process of cultural blindness: "More [plaques] were found . . . by the German Africanist Leo Frobenius, who attributed them to the heritage of Atlantis, the 'lost continent.' Other Europeans . . . thought these works of art must be of classical Greek lineage; or perhaps the creation of some solitary European of long ago who had arrived in Benin and conceived, by amazing genius, these 'un-African' masterpieces. Others again thought they were obvious products of the European Renaissance."

Later work by impartial archaeologists established beyond any doubt that the works found in Benin were produced between the 14th and 17th centuries and were indeed purely African. Without question, Benin's art developed directly from the Yoruba art of Ife, with one essential difference: whereas the Yoruba sculptors had worked in both terra-cotta and bronze, Benin's royal sculptors worked exclusively in bronze, an alloy of copper with tin and other metals. Humbler craftspeople often worked in other, locally available materials; among the great surviving works from Benin are a pair of carved ivory leopards whose spots are represented by inlaid bronze studs.

The shift to bronze occurred as copper became more readily available, first by way of North Africa and then through Portuguese traders. Benin's artists began by fashioning heads to adorn the altars of ancestors. As Benin became richer and grander, its sculptors began to create plaques to adorn the oba's palace. The plaques depicted a wide variety of subjects: obas with their vassals, religious rituals, musicians, birds, lizards, fish, and other images from nature. The art historian Jean Laude has written in *The Arts of Black Africa* that some degree of foreign influence may not, after all, have been entirely absent from the process of creation. "The forms of the plaques and the efforts of the artists to achieve a certain degree of perspective suggest that these works were inspired by engravings

The oba's palace in Benin City was adorned with bronze plaques portraying such diverse subjects as animals, musicians, soldiers, and figures of the royal court. In this fragment, a court musician beats a drum.

in illustrated European books which the artists had in their possession. But even if this hypothesis should be verified, it must be remembered that the pursuit of illusionistic effects and perspective is related to a psychological mode of apprehending the world and man: the concept of a stable and measurable space as the location of human activity or a spectacular setting for it. This concept is unique to Africa."

No one who looks at these works today can fail to perceive the qualities that set them apart from the art of any other culture—or doubt the splendor of the civilization that produced them.

8

UNDER THE KUMA TREE

✳

IN the chaos following the decline of ancient Ghana around the beginning of the 13th century, many groups of farmers moved south to the forestlands in search of refuge. Among these groups were the Akan, who settled in the region around the Volta River, in what is now the nation of Ghana. In this new home the Akan soon discovered one of West Africa's largest goldfields, and as they grew more affluent through trade in the precious metal, they formed a number of small states based upon descent lines.

Sometime after 1600, a group of Akan farmers from the coastal town of Adansi moved northward in search of more land and a share of the gold trade. Settling near a small lake in the forestland, they built the state of Asantemanso. As this new trade center

---

This wooden doll, with its narrow body, long neck, and large, flattened head, is known as an akuaba. In Asante, pregnant women carried such figures to ensure easy childbirth and beautiful children.

grew in wealth, other groups from Adansi moved north to join their former townspeople, and the people of Asantemanso and the surrounding region came to call themselves the Asante.

Though they had succeeded in bettering their lot, the Asante were still not in the forefront of the Akan peoples. In fact, the nearby state of Denkyira controlled many of their activities, charging them heavy taxes and forcing them to produce a certain number of slaves each year. The Asante's only hope of real progress lay in uniting their various communities, but until around the close of the 17th century, this goal remained elusive. In the end, the key to Asante unity turned out to be religion—the same force that had formed the basis of so many social institutions in Africa.

An Asante king named Osei Tutu, who came to power around 1695, discovered a way to use his people's spiritual beliefs to draw them together. His approach centered on the Asante's traditional symbol of leadership: the *akonnua,* or royal stool. The most important element in the Asante's kingship ceremony was the moment when a new monarch took possession of the akonnua, swearing his fidelity to the people and pledging to serve all the Asante rather than his own particular descent line.

After he had completed this ceremony, Osei Tutu called an assembly of the Asante people. The various chiefs and representatives were addressed by Osei Tutu's ally, an *okomfo* (priest) named Anokye. Anokye produced another akonnua, this one partially covered in gold, and placed it on Osei Tutu's knees. The Golden Stool,

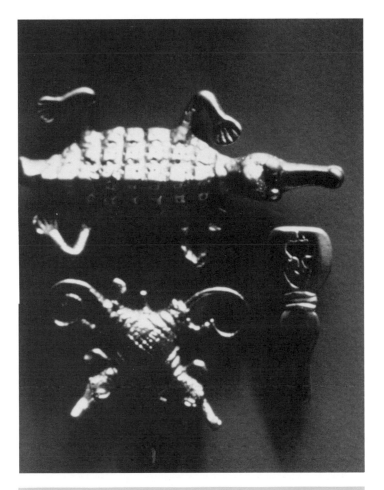

Asante traders used these decorative brass weights to measure gold dust.

Anokye told the people, had come down from the sky at the will of Nyame, the principal god of the Akan; it contained the soul of the Asante, and it was Nyame's desire that the Asante unite and become a great people. But they could only accomplish this by following the anointed guardian of the Golden Stool, Osei Tutu.

Osei Tutu had astutely called the assembly at a time when the Asante were under political and military pressure, and the people were prepared to accept the symbolic importance of the Golden Stool, to put aside their separate interests and work for the well-being of the nation. As soon as Osei Tutu had secured this promise, he took steps to ensure that the Asante union would not dissolve as quickly as past alliances. For example, he established a law that made it a crime for any of the Asante to speak about the history of his or her own group; instead, everyone had to speak of the Asante people as a whole. "'Ritual' and 'politics,' here as elsewhere, marched hand in hand," Basil Davidson wrote of this process. "Whether as the Golden Stool, the sacred spears of Central African kings, or the crown and sceptre of the monarchs of Europe, possession of the royal regalia provided the ultimate justification of political action. They were seen as the decisive instruments for transforming powers gained by superior force, intrigue, or good fortune into moral rights peculiar to the king."

Osei Tutu went on to rule the Asante until his death in 1717. He well understood that unity was meaningless without strength, and he immediately built up the Asante army by dividing it into four sections corresponding to the corners of a square: left, right, front, and rear. The head of an Asante state was appointed to command each section, and all the Asante warriors were assigned to one section or another on the basis of geography.

His army thus organized, Osei Tutu set out to defeat Denkyira in battle. For a time Bosianti, the king of Denkyira, was able to negotiate with Osei Tutu and forestall what he knew would be a costly war. He argued that the Asante and the people of Denkyira could do far better by cooperating than by fighting. Bosianti offered to release the Asante states from part of their obligation to provide gold and slaves. He also promised to help the Asante buy guns from the Dutch traders who were operating from the city of Elmina on the coast.

Though Osei Tutu did not really have faith in

Bosianti's offer of friendship, the conciliatory attitude of Denkyira kept him from going to war for many years. But when Bosianti was replaced by a new ruler who demanded heavier taxes from the Asante, Osei Tutu took the field. At first the Asante suffered heavy losses at the hands of the seasoned Denkyira forces, but in the end their efficient military organization carried the day. By 1701 they had subdued Denkyira's troops and gained control of much Denkyira territory. Among the possessions that fell into their hands was a trading contract with the Dutch. This document gave the Asante direct access to the Europeans, and its procurement was to have important consequences.

Before these consequences could unfold, the Asante confronted the task of empire building. Much of their territorial expansion was directed by Opoku Ware, who became king around 1720 and ruled for 30 years. His first challenge was to defeat a combined force of enemy states, including Denkyira, Sefwi, and Akwapim—a task he accomplished only after two bloody wars in which the Asante capital of Kumasi was temporarily captured. Opoku Ware went on to conquer a number of other neighboring states, such as Banda, Gonja, and Dagomba. By the late 1740s, Asante controlled the trade routes of the Middle Niger region.

During the second half of the 18th century and into the 19th century, Asante remained the supreme power in the region. Kings such as Osei Kwadwo (1764–77) added more territory through military conquest and made important reforms in government. Like other imperial peoples, the Asante found that they could not manage their complicated affairs through a handful of high-born administrators. Osei Kwadwo, therefore, began the practice of appointing outstanding individuals to important posts, regardless of their social station, and this program was followed by his successors right into the 19th century. In one

In 1817, members of a European expedition visiting Kumasi marveled at the wealth and magnificence of the Asante royal court. This painting by an expedition artist documents an Asante yam festival.

instance, a man who had begun as a salt carrier rose to the post of minister of foreign affairs. The rulers of Asante kept in touch with their officials through a complex network of messengers, and they also employed Muslim clerks to keep careful records of government affairs—thus they avoided the problems faced by the Yoruba rulers of Oyo, who communicated only by word of mouth.

The kings of Asante also followed the example of other rulers by maintaining a standing army. These troops, known as the Ankobia, were based in Kumasi and were specially designated to maintain order, both within the city and within the empire. Whenever there were signs of revolt among Asante's subject states, the Ankobia could be speedily dispatched to quell the disturbance.

Given the attention to detail displayed by Asante's rulers, it is not surprising that Kumasi—founded, according to Asante tradition, under a sacred tree known as the *kuma*—presented a splendid spectacle to visitors. Even a group of fastidious European traders who traveled to Kumasi in 1817 were impressed by the neatness of the streets and houses and the careful program of sanitation followed by the residents. They also discovered, as 5,000 of Kumasi's 40,000 citizens came out to greet them, that the people of Asante had brought their civilization to a high degree of style and enthusiasm:

> What we had seen on our way [wrote the Englishman William Bowditch] had made us expect something unusual. But we were still surprised by the extent and display of the scene which burst upon us here. An area of nearly a mile in circumference was crowded with magnificence and novelty. The king, his chiefs and captains, were splendidly dressed, and were surrounded by attendants of every kind. More than a hundred bands broke into music on our arrival. At least a hundred large umbrellas, each of which could shelter thirty persons, were sprung up and down by their bearers with a brilliant effect, being made in scarlet, yellow and the brightest cloths and silks, and crowned on top with crescents, pelicans, elephants, barrels, arms and swords of gold.

Such ornaments were just a sample of the Asante's artistic skills. Many of their most striking artifacts were fashioned not from bronze but from gold-plated alloys (combinations of metals), using the forgotten technique of lost-wax casting. As Jean Laude has indicated, the practice of making royal funeral masks and pendant masks most likely originated during the reign of Opoku Ware in the first half of the 18th century and was associated with Akan religious be-

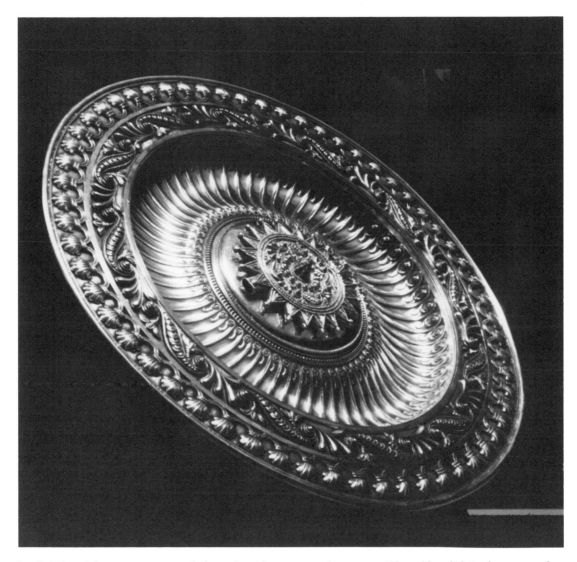

liefs. The Akan maintained that the *okra*, or soul, was divided into two parts: one represented the spirit of the individual and the other a separate being that would watch over him or her through eternity. "Round gold plaques worn on the chest," Laude wrote, "are the soul carriers. Only the bearer of the king's soul (*okrafo*), who had to belong to the sovereign's family, was entitled to wear them. The commemorative masks probably portrayed chiefs or kings killed or

The golden disk in the center of this plate was made to be worn on the chest of an okrafo, *the bearer of an Asante king's soul.*

British soldiers and Asante warriors fight for control of the Gold Coast in 1824. The Asante won this battle, but 50 years later another conflict with the British forced them to relinquish their land.

made prisoners in war. The motif sculpted at the corners of the lips symbolizes the soul (*honhom*) which escapes through the mouth at the moment of death. The Ashanti kings . . . continue to live in Heaven after death. From that vantage point they watch over their people. Golden masks placed on royal tombs prove the permanence of this invisible royalty."

Ultimately, the same Europeans who were so impressed with the achievements of the Asante were to
bring about the downfall of the empire. The visit of
the trading delegation in 1817 convinced the British
government that Asante was a rich source of trade,
and the government took over the coastal forts from
private trading companies in 1821. The Asante

Asante dignitaries carry their staffs of office during a ceremony in modern Ghana, where, despite 57 years of British rule, West African traditions live on.

quickly found cause to resent British policies along the coast: the British made their own arrangements with Asante's subject states, thus weakening the control of the empire.

Nevertheless, the Asante initially tried to tolerate the intruders. As Basil Davidson wrote, "The general approach . . . was to show enough strength to contain European ambitions within what were regarded as reasonable or inevitable limits, and then to make treaties of trade and friendship which, it was hoped, the Europeans would keep. Useful variations on this policy were found in playing off one set of Europeans against another. The kings only fought when all else failed."

The Asante were forced to go to war in 1824, when the British governor, Sir Charles McCarthy, launched a campaign intended to break their grip on the region. The Asante soundly defeated the British, sending McCarthy to his death. For the next half century, the British government steered clear of direct involvement in Asante, while British merchants kept peace with the empire and made vast sums from their holdings along the coast.

Ultimately, the competing empires of Britain and Asante were bound to face each other down. In 1872, the king of Asante sent an expedition to the coast to subdue the defiant vassal states allied with the British. General Tia, the commander of the expedition, at first attempted to negotiate with the British governor, Sir Garnet Wolseley. Tia assured Wolseley that there could be peace between Asante and Britain, if only the British would stop supporting the vassal states (including the always-troublesome Denkyira). Wolseley's response, in 1874, was to begin a full-scale invasion of Asante, which the battle-hardened veteran later called "the most horrible war I ever took part in." With great difficulty, the British forces finally occupied Kumasi and forced the Asante to sign the Treaty of Fomena, which guaranteed the British a free hand along the coast. The Asante rebuilt their ruined capital and attempted to resurrect their empire, but their efforts were finally ended by another British invasion in 1900. The Asante then became subjects of the British Empire and did not regain their independence until the nation of Ghana was formed in 1957.

In all these confrontations with the powers of Europe, the Africans were at a disadvantage because they could not match the technology and political flexibility that Europeans had developed since the end of the Middle Ages in 1500. There are many reasons for this disparity. One is surely the damage done to Africa by the slave trade and the enrichment of the nations that ran it.

On a deeper level, African and European societies were fundamentally different. Simply put, Africans had always remained close to the expansive continent they and their ancestors had tamed, and they believed deeply that their way of life could not be improved on. Africans, Basil Davidson has written, "were the victims of their own success. . . . Towards all questions of fundamental change they showed a fundamental hostility. They were conservative by the strictest definition. . . . Although the outcome of a great deal of daring experiment in the past, they had reached a self-perpetuating level where further large experiment seemed not only unwise, but also, given the spiritual sanctions that helped to stay them up, positively wrong."

Davidson adds that Africa's great political diversity became a fatal handicap in the face of such challenges as the slave trade and colonialism. Africans were completely unprepared to unite against a common enemy; it had never occurred to them that their entire way of life could be threatened by outside forces. They and their ancestors had tamed a vast and beautiful continent that provided them with everything they desired. They had never felt the need, as Europeans had, to build ships and sail out to see what lay beyond the horizon. Confronted by aggressive intruders who had developed the ambition and the tools to remake the world in their own image, the peoples of Africa had little hope of preserving what they had so carefully built up.

With the fall of Asante, the last of the great West African kingdoms faded from view. Africa would have to endure decades of colonial rule before Africans' quest for nationhood became a political reality in the

20th century. Though they lie within different borders, the cities of the ancient kingdoms—Benin, Oyo,
Timbuktu, Jenne, Gao, Kumasi—endure, living relics
of a glorious heritage.

FURTHER READING

Battuta, Ibn. *Travels in Asia and Africa, 1325–1354*. Translated by H. A. R. Gibb. London: Routledge, 1957.

Connah, Graham. *African Civilizations*. Cambridge, England: Cambridge University Press, 1987.

Davidson, Basil. *Africa in History*. Rev. ed. New York: Collier, 1991.

———. *The African Genius*. Boston: Little, Brown, 1969.

———. *Lost Cities of Africa*. Rev. ed. Boston: Little, Brown, 1987.

Davidson, Basil, with F. K. Buah and J. F. A. Ajayi. *A History of West Africa: 1000–1600*. New rev. ed. London: Longman, 1977.

Fage, J. D. *An Atlas of African History*. London: Edward Arnold, 1978.

Hourani, Albert. *A History of the Arab Peoples*. New York: Warner Books, 1991.

Hrbek, I., ed. *Africa from the Seventh to the Eleventh Century*. Vol. 3. *UNESCO General History of Africa*. Abr. ed. Berkeley: University of California Press, 1992.

Hull, Richard W. *African Cities and Towns Before the European Conquest*. New York: Norton, 1976.

Laude, Jean. *The Arts of Black Africa*. Translated by Jean Decock. Berkeley: University of California Press, 1971.

Levtzion, Nehemiah. *Ancient Ghana and Mali*. New York: Africana, 1980.

Levtzion, Nehemiah, and J. F. G. Hopkins. *Corpus of Early Arabic Sources for West African History*. Cambridge, England: Cambridge University Press, 1981.

McLeod, Malcolm D. *The Asante*. London: British Museum Press, 1981.

Oliver, Roland, and Anthony Atmore. *Africa Since 1800*. 3rd ed. Cambridge, England: Cambridge University Press, 1981.

Oliver, Roland, and B. M. Fagan. *Africa in the Iron Age*. Cambridge, England: Cambridge University Press, 1975.

Oliver, Roland, and J. D. Fage. *A Short History of Africa*. 6th ed. New York: Penguin, 1988.

Previté-Orton, C. W. *The Shorter Cambridge Medieval History*. 2 vols. Cambridge, England: Cambridge University Press, 1952.

INDEX

Sebastian (king of Portugal), 58
Sefawa dynasty, 62, 63, 64
Sefawa empire, 61–65. *See also* Kanem-Bornu
Sefwi, 103
Senegal River, 25, 38
Shekkaru, 65, 66
Slavery, 67, 82, 83, 90–94, 100, 102, 112
Songhay, the, 49, 50
Songhay empire, 49–59, 63, 67
Soninke, the, 25, 26, 27
Soso, the, 37
Spain, 33, 34, 89
Stone Age, 16, 18, 19, 73, 76
Sudan, 37, 44, 47, 50, 59, 61, 64, 69, 70, 76, 81

Sultan Muhammad Bello, 71, 82
Sumanguru, 37, 38, 39
Sundiata Keita (king of Mali), 39–40, 41, 50
Sunni Ali (king of Songhay), 49–51, 54, 55
Sunni Baru (king of Songhay), 51–52

Takrur, 34, 37
Tallensi, the, 75
Tanzania, 13
Tarikh al Fattash (Muhammad Kati), 55
Teghaza, 55, 58
Timbuktu, 42, 43, 47, 50, 51, 52, 54, 55, 56, 59, 113
Tondibi, Battle of, 59

Tuareg, the, 46, 50, 51, 54, 70
Tunka Manin (king of Ghana), 28, 31

Uthman Dan Fodio, 64, 70
Volta River, 99
Wagadu, 25. *See also* Ghana, ancient
Walata, 38, 45, 47
West Africa, 20, 21, 23, 25, 30, 31, 40, 42, 49, 51, 54, 55, 57, 66, 67, 76, 86, 90, 91, 92, 93
Wolof, the, 47
Wolseley, Sir Garnet, 111

Yoruba, the, 67, 75–83, 85, 95, 104
Yusuf ibn Tashufin, 34

PICTURE CREDITS

The Bettmann Archive: pp. 20–21, 24–25, 29, 62, 68, 74, 108–9; Bridgeman Art Library/Art Resource, NY: p. 87; Courtesy Department of Library Services, American Museum of Natural History: pp. 14–15 (neg. #335273), 17 (neg. #411258), 66 (neg. #338387), 72–73 (neg. #325338), 78 (neg. #325536), 101 (neg. #338386), 104–5 (neg. #337395), 107 (neg. #338388); Werner Forman Archive/Art Resource, NY: cover, pp. 12–13, 18, 32, 36–37, 38, 41, 44, 48–49, 53, 56, 57, 60–61, 76, 77, 81, 84–85, 89, 91, 92, 96; Giraudon/Art Resource, NY: p. 2; Sassoonian/Art Resource, NY: pp. 98–99; UPI/Bettmann: pp. 26, 110.
Map (p. 58) by Gary Tong.

PHILIP KOSLOW earned his B.A. and M.A. degrees from New York University and went on to teach and conduct research at Oxford University, where his long-standing interest in medieval European and African history was awakened. The editor of numerous volumes for young readers, he is also the author of *El Cid* in the Chelsea House HISPANICS OF ACHIEVEMENT series and of *The Seminole Indians* in Chelsea House's JUNIOR LIBRARY OF AMERICAN INDIANS. Koslow is currently at work on a comprehensive 10-volume series on the kingdoms of West Africa.

CLAYBORNE CARSON, senior consulting editor of the MILESTONES IN BLACK AMERICAN HISTORY series, is a professor of history at Stanford University. His first book, *In Struggle: SNCC and the Black Awakening of the 1960s* (1981), won the Frederick Jackson Turner Prize of the Organization of American Historians. He is the director of the Martin Luther King, Jr., Papers Project, which will publish 12 volumes of King's writings.

DARLENE CLARK HINE, senior consulting editor of the MILESTONES IN BLACK AMERICAN HISTORY series, is the John A. Hannah Professor of American History at Michigan State University. She is the author of numerous books and articles on black women's history. Her most recent work is the two-volume *Black Women in America: An Historical Encyclopedia* (1993).